BONFIRE
OF
UREAUCRACY
IN EUROPE

DERK JAN EPPINK

BONFIRE
OF
BUREAUCRACY
IN EUROPE

Plea for a United Europe of States

LANNOO

www.lannoo.com

Register on our website and we will regularly send you a newsletter with information
about new books and interesting, exclusive offers.

Cover photo: Corbis
Design: Studio Lannoo
English translation: Ian Connerty

© Uitgeverij Lannoo nv, Tielt, 2010 and Derk Jan Eppink
D/2010/45/289 - ISBN 978 90 209 9093 5 - NUR 697

SUMMARY

INTRODUCTION

On June 7 2009, I was elected to a seat in the European Parliament. I was a cross-border candidate, a Dutchman who got elected for a Flemish party in Belgium. This was my fourth time in the Parliament, each time in a different capacity. I first went there in 1984 as a young, powerless but nonetheless dedicated assistant. During the 1990s, I worked there as a journalist, regularly covering European affairs. From 2000 to 2007, I was a member of the cabinet staff for two different European commissioners – five years for Frits Bolkestein and two and a half years for Siim Kallas, who is currently Vice-President of the European Commission. To put it bluntly, I regarded my election to the European Parliament as a 'return to the scene of the crime'. Europe's institutions have undergone great change during that period of 25 years. Since the beginning of the 1980s, the number of member states has grown from 10 to 27. European legislation touches almost every part of our daily lives. The European Parliament has acquired a degree of power that few rulers would dream of. Politicians come and politicians go, but the system continues to expand. In this book, I will describe the workings, growth and power of the European bureaucracy from the inside.

With this bird's eye view of the last 25 years of European history, I will also conduct an enquiry into the state of mind of the European elite, to which I too belong. I am not an outsider; admittedly I am an insider. I have no criticism of any specific person, since the system has now become much stronger than any mere individual. In Brussels, power is not vested in people but in institutions. The machine functions by itself and its human servants are each trapped inside their own little cocoon of activity. This machine has a huge weight, but there is no effective counterweight; there is no legitimate opposition, not even in the European Parliament. This allows the machine to steamroller forward. Whatever direction it chooses, one course is predominant: more bureaucracy, more regulation, more money and more Europe.

Nobody disputes the achievements of European integration. Without it the old continent would have been reduced to provincial status long ago. The overriding ideal of the wartime generation – namely, no more war – has been achieved, at least in Northern and Western Europe. My father was a forced labourer in the German war industry during the Second World War, working in the factories of the Ruhr. My grandparents and other members of my family would hide escaping British airmen and Jews, since as good Calvinists they considered that resistance to the crimes of an evil government was a moral duty. Many towns along the Dutch-German border were regularly bombed – albeit by accident – by Allied planes on their way to attack Germany's industrial heartland. But this historical background is very difficult to explain to a younger generation which never really knew what the Berlin Wall stood for and whose view of historical events is predominantly shaped by the Hollywood entertainment industry. This generation has a very different frame of reference. For them, stories about the war belong to 'grandad's time'. 'Modern' education has allowed our children to grow up in an historical vacuum. Our collective memory has faded away.

For this reason, Europe means something different to the members of each generation. For me, it was an enormous chance to broaden my horizons and to meet different people from different cultures. I have an international family – a Russian wife who is an interpreter at the United Nations – and children who are being raised in three different languages. At home, we have a choice of six passports, ranging from Dutch to Russian and American. I have no idea to what extent my children will ever feel themselves to be European. This book was largely written on an Indian Jet Airlines aeroplane flying above the Atlantic Ocean, as I commute twice a month from Brussels to New York. Airports are good meeting places for members of the European Parliament, rather like the village squares of an increasingly globalised world. We are somehow the new nomads and airplanes are our camels. Most of us even spend more time sitting in aeroplanes than in our own front rooms at home. It sounds cosmopolitan, but the potential estrangement – and in particular the cultural alienation – of the European elite is fraught with danger.

What will Europe be for my children? Will it just be an old continent, confined to the margins of world history? Or will it be something more? The next decade will be crucial for the future generations of Europeans. In particular, the 1968 generation bears a heavy responsibility. Its people received the best education and were given the best jobs, with the best salaries – and are now demanding the highest pensions ever. But they are also leaving behind them the highest ever levels of debt; a bill to be picked up by their children. Never before in the history of Western Europe has a single generation consumed so much to so little lasting purpose. They have been living on credit for far too long, so that the socio-economic foundations of Europe have been weakened, perhaps fatally. Does this mean that Europe is destined to become little more than the world's museum? Possibly. But this will not be enough to provide a living for more than 500 million people.

In the European fray of political ideas, two fundamental ideals often find themselves in opposition to each other. These are the 'ideal of freedom' and the 'ideal of equality'. 'Freedom' is the driving force behind progress, but for many people the inequalities in prosperity it tends to produce undermines its legitimacy. This swings the pendulum back in favour of 'equality' which, if pushed to its limit, becomes economically unsustainable. The European ideal – the dream of a continent without war, reconciliation between peoples, a large measure of cooperation between nation states to achieve prosperity for all – balances on a knife edge between these two contrasting and conflicting philosophies. A balance not properly struck, irrespective of good intentions or well-defined aims, is tantamount to political disaster, of which Europe has had its share.

Initially, freedom gained the upper hand. The original European Community was based on the four classic economic freedoms: the free movement of goods, services, capital and labour. Europe had to become a free zone, where economic growth and prosperity could flourish. This was the dream of the wartime generation. The creation of the European Iron and Steel Community was intended to prevent the future development of a war economy, and the Common Agricultural Policy was designed to secure the independence of adequate food production across the six member states. These goals were achieved. Europe recovered from the ravages of war and reached a new level of prosperity that the pre-war generation could scarcely imagine.

With the growth of the welfare state in Western Europe, equality also started to gain ground in the Community's thinking. The European Community (EC) not only began to extend its geographical frontiers, but also acquired an increasing number of new tasks. Europe laid the basis for a regional policy, a cohesion policy, a social policy and an employment policy. Structural funds were created, which distributed a wide range of subsidies in keeping with the principle of equality. There was a perceived need for European 'convergence by solidarity'. In 1992, with this aim in mind, the European Community was reborn as the European Union (EU), with the clear idea that this must become a political entity. The emphasis was now shifted firmly from freedom to equality: greater equality within Europe and greater equality between Europe and the Third World.

There is an important difference between the <u>freedom ideal and the equality ideal</u>: freedom allows for limited government whereas equality invariably requires big government. The European freedom ideal envisaged the elimination of restrictive rules and regulations and promoted a level playing field on which countries would be given an equal chance to develop. Europe created the framework within which goods, services, capital and labour could move freely – and therefore be put to best use. Brussels – as is still the case today – saw its task as fighting against Member States that still dared to engage in restrictive practices to protect their own markets. By 1992, it seemed that the internal market had been achieved, but in reality the playing field was never as level as it seemed.

The equality ideal works in a different manner: a detailed system of European regulations and subsidy funds are used to compel a form of equality. Europe's legislators are active in many different fields to ensure that this principle of equality is applied. Europe's subsidy funds circulate money around the continent to promote convergence. The end result is more money but also more bureaucracy. This is the Achilles Heel of the present day European Union. The desire for greater equality necessitates more funding which generates still more bureaucracy and the need for more financial resources. It is a vicious circle that is difficult to break.

In reality, the 'more money' side of the equation is of 'relative value', since the economic success of a Member State within the Union is mainly dependent upon its fiscal and economic policy; not upon EU generosity. If a Member State introduces a high level of taxation and follows a policy which is unfavourable to investment opportunities, it can reap few benefits. In that case, the rich supply of European funding does not help. It is money thrown away. If, on the other hand, the policy stimulates investment, through a system of fiscal benefits, the Member State will achieve growth. European subsidies are merely a nice financial 'nudge in the back'. Ireland and Spain were economic backwaters when they entered the European Community. They created wealth by opening markets, liberalising utility sectors and embracing foreign investment; European subsidies were just a bit of extra help. It was nothing more than that. But in accordance with the widely preached 'equality principle', the European bureaucracy perceives the stream of funding as an 'absolute value'. It regards 'convergence' as a process steered from the top. Brussels portrays itself as the do-gooder in chief, the unique source of benevolence and the main force of civilisation in the world. The bureaucrats congratulate themselves on this happy state of affairs and demand more of the same. Europeans in poor areas or countries should be grateful to them and pay due respect.

Inevitably, there comes a moment when equality begins to supersede freedom, with all the negative consequences that this implies. The European bureaucracy continues to grow and launches – often with the best of intentions – tier after tier of new legislation, resulting in micromanagement of the worst kind. Economic sectors are swamped by overregulation, the subsidy stream increases and the citizens of Europe watch open-mouthed as the many-headed hydra of Brussels grows ever more powerful, crushing human inventiveness – the very foundation of the freedom ideal – beneath its scaly feet. Gradually, equality starts to crowd out freedom. No matter how noble the aim, the economic result is in inverse proportion to the political objective. The ultimate consequence is bureaucratic overreach, both in European welfare states and in the European Union, accompanied by economic stagnation, monetary chaos and the redistribution of poverty.

In short, Europe needs to reinvent itself. It needs to revive and revitalise itself, to change its mental outlook. It needs to bring an end to the seemingly endless flow of bureaucracy and subsidies. Europe will not be saved by new administrative guidelines and new regional development funds. No one in Brussels is willing to call a halt to this madness – and so the European taxpayers will have to do it. The 'ordinary' people of Europe will have to cry: "enough is enough!" It will be like a capitalist version of Marxism: "Taxpayers of Europe unite: you have nothing to lose but your chains!"

This must entail a political adjustment: a new shift away from equality back towards freedom. It must involve a new appeal, not to the mandarins in Brussels, but to the resilience of its peoples in all their diversity. Freedom and human initiative must once again become the driving forces behind European innovation, enterprise and production. Taxes must be reduced, good work should be rewarded, outstanding service honoured. New technologies must be stimulated, even if this leads to inequalities in income. Freedom leads to inequalities and to envy, but it also produces the growth that Europe now so desperately needs as its only hope for economic survival.

This is why I plead for a Europe that will once again focus on its most essential core task – the sustainable prosperity of its 500 million inhabitants. It is a last-ditch effort all Europeans should make because the alternative is economic desertification and historic oblivion.

1

AN EVER PROUDER PARLIAMENT

If European federalism is a religion, then the European Parliament is its cathedral. When, on the day of my swearing in, I had finally found my allocated office on the thirteenth floor of the Louise Weiss Building – a very small office, but with a stunning view over the Rhine Delta and the Black Forest – the first thing I did was to turn on the television. The eyes of almost every station were focused on Europe, and, in particular, on the Plenary Chamber of the European Parliament, the epicentre of European democracy. The 'old' parliament was rounding off its final day in session. I expected that there would be some sort of farewell reception, perhaps with a glass of champagne, or maybe even two. But I was mistaken. Instead, what I saw was an almost bewildering, if not ludicrous spectacle, but one that says much about the European Union.

The President of the Parliament, Hans Gert Pöttering, was dishing out medals to the European Members of Parliament (MEPs) who would not be returning when the new parliament convened, either because they were retiring or because they had not been re-elected. Pöttering, himself an MEP since the first direct European elections in 1979, received his departing colleagues in a manner that reminded me of a papal audience in Rome. One by one, they shuffled forward, waiting for their turn to be congratulated by their President. After lots of warm handshaking, and sometimes even an embrace, they were handed their medal for 'services rendered'. Pöttering and his team looked and behaved as though they were standing at a crossroads in history, like a latter day Christopher Columbus and his crew, destined to lead the people of Europe to the New

World. And perhaps they really did think that they had altered the course of history, and that their work was essential for the continued well-being – perhaps even the survival – of the old continent. They certainly all shared the 'European conviction', even though they might be hard-pressed to explain exactly what this means. Is it some kind of mutual congratulation society for European politicians; is it a general feeling of shared destiny; or is it simply a European variant of the American Dream? In the European Parliament, the term 'European conviction' – no matter how poorly defined – is an important concept. Every candidate for the position of European Commissioner is grilled remorselessly by the Parliament to see whether or not he (or she) possesses this indispensible quality. If they fail to find it, the candidate risks being branded as 'anti-European' and will probably be rejected. From then on, they are labelled as 'an enemy of Europe'.

The day before my swearing-in, the blue European flag was raised in a ceremony that was almost military. On the day itself, the new President of the Parliament was duly elected and the European anthem – Beethoven's *Ode to Joy* – sounded through the 736-seat Plenary Chamber at a deafening level. Most of the members stood to attention, with a far-off, misty look in their eyes: the look of the visionary. Yet the flag and the anthem were the symbols of a European constitution which was ultimately rejected by the peoples of Europe. The symbolism was later dropped and did not reappear in the Treaty of Lisbon, which was effectively a watered-down version of the original constitutional draft. Even so, the European Parliament continues to live on in the spirit of this now defunct constitution. Perhaps the 'European conviction' is a kind of secular faith for the 21st century, a religion without God: Europe serving as *Erstatzreligion*.

It is noticeable that in a Europe that is now largely de-Christianised, secular matters are being increasingly used to fill the unseemly but nonetheless persistent need to believe in something. But how is a sober, ritual-free Calvinist supposed to react to all this? My new parliamentary colleagues soon told me. I was supposed to think that I was now a part of 'something special', that I was privileged to participate in a 'sacred mission', that I was witnessing a unique moment in the history of Europe. In short, I was now a bit-player in the creation of a new Europe, although the creation story seemed to be lasting a lot longer than the original seven-day biblical version. I was supposed to feel as if I belonged to some kind of political avantgarde – one of the chosen few, standing Moses-like atop our fictive Strasbourg Mountain, gazing into the distance at the Promised Land. So far, all I could see was the Rhine Delta and the Black Forest. A nice enough view, and symbolic, too, for Europeans, with the Franco-German border running through it. But could this really be the Promised Land? Nobody really knows what the Promised Land looks like or where it is, but it was clear to me that we, the representatives of the European Parliament, were expected – and intended – to lead our people there, if need be against their will.

Because in reality, the European Parliament has exactly the same problem as Moses had: the people can sometimes be difficult. Some want to reach the Promised Land by their own route, while others refuse to believe that the land of milk and honey even exists. They moan and groan about the great ideal that is supposed to bring collective happiness to everyone. And the MEPs don't even have to go very far to have this dissatisfaction confirmed. Just a few streets away from the parliament building in Strasbourg, you can find hundreds of 'Europeans', who speak with total indifference about the great 'creative' experiment. The only people who are really keen on it are the taxi-drivers and the restaurant owners, but their interest is commercial rather than ideological. This simply reflects the huge gap between the mindset of the European Parliament and the 'street' – in whatever country of Europe.

In fact, in many countries this feeling of general indifference is gradually being transformed into active resistance, even rebellion. An increasing number of Europeans see Europe as a threat to their own identity. When the European Parliament was directly elected for the first time in 1979, it was assumed that growing public support would eventually lead to it acquiring greater powers. In the meantime, these powers have indeed been acquired and the MEPs now have more 'clout' than their colleagues in Belgium and France combined. But this has not happened because of growing public support. On the contrary, this has fallen consistently. For the 1979 election, the average turnout across Europe was 61.9%. In 2009, just 43% of Europeans could be bothered to turn up at the polls. In other words, the majority of Europeans chose not to vote. The turn-out rate in key European countries such as Germany, France, The Netherlands and Italy has fallen by more than 20%. Great Britain is one of the few countries where the rate has actually increased: from an apathetic 32.3% in 1979 to the dizzy heights of an abysmal 34.7% in 2009!

This would suggest – putting it mildly – that large segments of the European population have their doubts about the 'European conviction'. They are not convinced by the new creation story peddled by Strasbourg and Brussels. They question the content of various aspects of the 'sacred mission'. They consider the European Union to be too expensive or too bureaucratic. Or they just don't care. Pöttering is an icon in the European Parliament, but only 1% of Germans actually know who he is. Even your average footballer scores better than that!

MEPs are assumed to be pro-European: people who believe in the 'conviction' in its purest form. As a result, the represent-atives of the more critical Europeans are very much the odd-men-out in the parliament. For the parliamentary 'believers', these men and women are labelled as 'anti-European' or 'Euro-sceptics', simply because they dare to challenge the 'official' ideology. They are, in fact, the heretics of the European church, even though they have been duly chosen by the democratic process. They are considered elected heretics.

The European creation story has its own political ideology: the *ever closer Union*. These words were already included in the original 1958 Treaty of Rome, but they were imbued with deeper significance in the 1992 Treaty of Maastricht, when the European Community was re-baptised as the European Union and the euro was designed to become the basis for Economic and Monetary Union. This was the moment when the EU became a true political entity. Moreover, this Union is not just any ordinary union: it is an *ever closer Union*. According to the philosophy of this union – of which the European Parliament is the self-appointed protector – Europe will continue to grow organically towards closer Political Union in a historically irreversible process. This means, in turn, that ever-increasing amounts of money, personnel and resources will flow towards Brussels, thereby underpinning the European structure as a whole. Every new treaty or every new summit meeting must therefore result in 'more Europe'. Every new guideline, every new institution or agency is a step towards the Promised Land. Originally, the European Community is a venture of cooperation between nations who voluntarily agreed to surrender a limited part of their sovereignty. But Maastricht gave the new Europe a mission. And the new missionaries were the European parliamentarians, treading the pilgrim path between Brussels and Strasbourg.

Part of this mission was to systematically undermine the national member states, so that a critical mass of power was shifted to Brussels. In other words, the Member States were no longer expected to surrender parts of their sovereignty voluntarily: they were to have them removed by legal means. As soon as a new problem arose – no matter what it was – the European Parliament would declare solemnly that it was a 'European problem', as a result of which the issue was transferred to the meeting tables of Brussels. In other words, the decisions were placed in the hands of the European elite – not in the hands of the people. The mission provided a mandate, as defined by the European elite itself.

In political and geographical terms, the concept of the *ever closer Union* is virtually unlimited. The Union grows both from within and on the outside. Brussels decides more and more and the Union grows exponentially. And because the process – right from the very beginning – has been portrayed as 'historically inevitable' (i.e., irreversible) nobody now dares to pose the question of where the final limits actually lie. And perish the thought that someone might suggest that Europe's huge resources should be reduced and perhaps even retransferred back to the national member states. This final suggestion is the ultimate sin – if not a crime – for the European faithful. Anyone who has the audacity to propose such a thing is clearly lacking in 'European conviction'. At best, they may simply be misguided, capable of reconversion. At worst, they may even be saboteurs! If they repent, they can be readmitted to the European fold, but if they persist in their wicked ways then they are clearly of 'bad faith' and will be consigned to the one of the darker pits of hell. The dogma of the *ever closer Union* allows no room for doubt or backsliding. "Those who are not for us, are against us." Would a cardinal suggest to the pope that perhaps God really doesn't exist after all? Would a communist leader suggest to his Politburo comrades that maybe Lenin had got hold of the wrong end of the stick? The cardinal would find himself in purgatory and the communist in Siberia quicker than you could say three 'Hail Mary's' or sing the International. If the orthodoxy of a belief is questioned, that belief is already on the slippery slope to ruin. As a result, these questions must never be posed. Or if they are posed, the person who poses them must be discredited as a heretic or a lunatic. Each year, the European Parliament awards the Sakharov Prize to encourage dissidents all over the world – but it refuses to tolerate dissidence within its own house.

Nevertheless, the time has now come when these questions need to be asked, even in a European Parliament which likes to see itself as the cathedral of orthodoxy. And the questions are not coming from so-called heretical MEPs, but from the peoples of Europe themselves, in whose name the Parliament is supposed to speak.

Every time the people want to say something, the mandarins in Brussels begin to get nervous. Anyone who dares to mention the word 'referendum' is branded as a 'populist'. On 12 January 2005, the European Parliament approved the European Constitution by a massive majority (500 for, 137 against and 40 abstentions), but within a year the people of France and the Netherlands, voting in national referenda, had rejected the constitution out of hand. Other Member States that were planning similar referenda quickly had them cancelled, to avoid further embarrassment to the European ideal.

In other words, as far as Europe is concerned, the tiresome public either doesn't turn up to vote, or, if it does, it usually votes in a manner calculated to raise the blood pressure of the European faithful. Clearly, there is a hiatus between the leaders of Europe and the peoples of Europe, to whom the European dogma is supposed to be applied. The leaders lead, but the people simply don't want to follow. And so the leaders complain – just like our old friend Moses – about the ingratitude of people. But is this really true? Are they really ungrateful? If so, then perhaps it is time to change the people, or alternatively their leaders?

The Treaty of Lisbon also experienced similar problems. Most European leaders did their best to avoid a referendum. However, the constitution in Ireland made a referendum mandatory – and the people voted 'no'. Brussels was angry, very angry. Those ungrateful Irish whiskey drinkers! They had made themselves rich on the back of European subsidies, and now they dared to put two fingers up – or one, depending on the country where you live – to the European ideal. The fact that Ireland became prosperous thanks to its own excellent climate of investment was quickly overlooked because this does not fit in with the prevailing Brussels ideology. Europe 'does things' for people, so it is not possible to concede that people might sometimes actually do things for themselves.

The troublesome Irish were eventually persuaded to vote a second time – but now with a gun to their head. There were ominous warnings from Brussels that a second 'no' vote would have harmful effects on the Irish economy. With a world recession looming, it was Hobson's choice: the Irish could either vote 'yes' or 'yes' – and so they voted 'yes'. But the troubles didn't stop there. For months the Czech President, Vaclav Klaus, also refused to sign the Treaty of Lisbon. This, not surprisingly, earned him the opprobrium of the European hierarchy. Yet another ungrateful troublemaker! One man who dared to stand in the way of Europe's destiny! Pressure was gradually applied and the stubborn Czech finally yielded – but not before he had earned his place in history as one of the few men to be detested in his time by both the Soviet Union and the European Union. This is true dissidence indeed – but I somehow doubt that he will ever be awarded the Sakharov Prize!

By now, Brussels was starting to get a bit tired of this sort of thing, and so they devised a method to deal with the dissidents once and for all. The revised Treaty of Lisbon included a provision that the EU can alter its own articles, providing all the Member States agree. This self-amendment clause is a handy way of avoiding referenda. And if the people no longer have a voice, then they can't say 'no'! Besides, it was now argued that the European treaties are much too complex for the ordinary public to understand: surely, it's a much better idea to leave it to the experts? This is not the kind of democratic theory you will find in Aristotle or Rousseau. In fact, it makes you wonder why we need to bother with elections at all.

It is a curious paradox that the European Parliament portrays itself as the defender of the *ever closer Union*, while the peoples of Europe are the greatest opponents of the EU's federal ideals. This suggests a serious lack of legitimacy, which has manifested itself on several occasions in the form of the unwillingness the European public to vote. Is there a lack of legitimacy? Not a bit of it! According to Brussels, the people consciously decide not to vote, because they are happy with the way things are going! The fact that the public is voting with its feet to protest constantly to the contrary seems to pass them by unnoticed.

All this can make life very difficult for your average European MEP. Inside the Plenary Chamber, they are sitting on roses and are treated like kings. Outside the Chamber, they are sitting on a bed of nettles, in particular when exposed to public opinion. If an MEP walks into a pub anywhere in Europe, he would be a brave man to actually reveal what he does for a living. Even a respected politician like Dutchman Piet Dankert (a past President of the European Parliament) was once accused in his local supermarket of being nothing more than a money-grabbing sponger, getting rich quick at the taxpayer's expense. This is not untypical. While the majority of Europe's politicians live in the ivory-tower atmosphere of self-congratulation, the outside world is becoming increasingly hostile. Public indifference with Europe is gradually turning to public anger and public mistrust. This is reflected in the fact that the European Parliament now contains a number of groupings which are actively hostile to the orthodoxy of the *ever closer Union*. Some of them want to return to the status quo ante of the old *Common Market* days. Against the background of the Treaty of Lisbon, this is an unrealistic objective, but it is at least indicative of the growing level of public discontent.

Are these new radical groupings just a temporary phenomenon, or are they the beginning of a new trend in European politics? In the Plenary Chamber, the European believers regard them – and treat them – as pariahs. However, they have been elected by due democratic process and therefore they have the right to speak, provided they speak decently. An avalanche begins with the disturbance of just a single, tiny stone. Will these growing voices of protest one day cause that avalanche? It certainly seems likely that the current political situation will be untenable in the long term. A European Parliament which defends the European ideal with missionary-like zeal is simply not compatible with a European public which has lost its faith. The Brussels bureaucracy thinks that the European machine can carry on regardless, even if nobody turns up to vote in its elections. But this is simply another example of wishful thinking. Long before the 0% threshold is reached, public indifference will have exploded in public revolt, with the Berlaymont Building in Brussels – the headquarters of the European Commission – or the Paul Henri Spaak Building of the European Parliament cast as the new Bastilles of the 21st century.

The second major problem with the *ever closer Union* might be described as a theological one. In Brussels, there is a growing belief in the Political Union as a kind of panacea, a universal means to solve all our continent's problems, no matter how big the EU becomes. It is rooted in the overriding view that there is simply no alternative to the *ever closer Union*, except an unacceptable form of political obscurantism. Political Union, it is said, will automatically lead to more growth, more prosperity and more employment in Europe, allowing the EU to remain a major player on the world stage. For this reason, every alternative proposal to the *ever closer Union* is depicted as being a historically outmoded form of provincialism, or as the Germans say, *Kleinstaaterei*. But is this really true? Yet again, in the corridors of Brussels and Strasbourg it is almost a criminal act to suggest such a thing. In reality, however, there are many problems for which the European Union currently does not have an answer and the EU is carrying less and less weight in the international arena, notwithstanding the endless attempts to create 'more Europe'.

If we place Europe on a time line, it should be clear to everyone that the EU is not working towards a flourishing, optimistic and energetic future. On the contrary, Europe is currently managing its own decline. It may be possible to slow down the rate of this decline, but it cannot be held back indefinitely. The financial and economic crisis has already increased the pace of our fall, with huge budget deficits and mounting national debt as a result. For the time being, most Europeans are not yet feeling the effects of this worsening situation in their daily life, but by the time they realise how late it is, the damage will already have been done.

Moreover, it is difficult to avoid the conclusion that, with the exception of trade, the European Union has currently very little influence at world level. In the next decade the fulcrum of economic power will shift decisively from the Atlantic to the Pacific Basin: From Europe to Asia, with America in between, just about holding its own. This will inevitably mean the end of

Euro-centrism, which is still such an important part of the thinking of the European elite.

After centuries of standing at the centre of the world, Europe will gradually be edged to its periphery. Europe's share in world trade fell from 19% in 2002 to 17.5% in 2007. During the same period, China's share increased from 7.2% to 12.3%. During the next ten years, it is predicted that China and the European Union will switch places. This will make China the world's largest economy, after the United States. India will become the sixth largest economy, taking the place currently occupied by France.

At the same time, continuing demographic decline in Europe, combined with new waves of migration, will result in an economic and cultural transformation of the old continent. The population will become older and less productive. In particular, Germany and Italy are struggling to deal with the problem of a shrinking population, while all European countries are faced with the prospect of a much smaller work force and a much larger group of pensioners. Of the major European nations, only France and Great Britain are keeping their heads above the demographic waves. But the general picture is alarming. In 2010, 25.9% of the population in the 27 EU member states is older than 65 years of age. By 2020, this figure will have risen to 31.5%. And so it goes on. According to some pundits, by 2050 a staggering 50% of all Europe's citizens will have reached pensionable age. In Poland this will be 55.7%, in Germany 56.4%, in Spain 58.9% and in Italy – the champion in the 'oldies' league – 59.2%. The Italians – including their prime minister – are always singing about *amore*, but they would do better to apply some of it before it is too late! The tipping point in the ageing of our population is likely to be reached in the course of this decade. The statistics paint a picture not dissimilar to a demographic 'Euro hockey stick'. In comparison, America's population will grow from its current 314 million to 500 million by the year 2050, with both the population of European descent and the newcomers from Latin America making equal contributions.

The increasing influx into Europe of newcomers from Islamic countries is also likely to heighten the continent's problems, not only in economic terms but also in terms of a potential clash of values. This clash is likely to be focused in three specific areas: freedom of expression, freedom of religion and equality between men and women. While ageing is threatening to bring about the collapse of Europe's traditional social welfare systems, migration is threatening to overwhelm Europe's metropolitan infrastructure. The rapidly increasing birth rate in Africa, particularly in the Maghreb countries, is likely to impose a permanent immigration strain on the lands of the European Union. In 2010, the population of North Africa – from Egypt to Morocco – is some 213 million. By 2020, this figure will have risen to 247.5 million and by 2050 to 321 million. But in contrast to Europe, in 2020 just 5.8% of North Africans will be aged 65 or over. In other words, North Africa is packed with young people, very few of whom have economic prospects. You don't need to be a Malthus to work out where all these people are likely to go.

Can Europe deal with immigration on a massive scale without a parallel process of integration? I do not think so. If no such process is forthcoming, the likely result is economic stagnation and socio-cultural tension. And what would happen to the euro in such a potentially volatile situation? The euro is already under considerable pressure as a result of the EU's budget deficits, which are only likely to become more burdensome as time passes. The difficulties in Greece are just a sign of things to come. Spain is also locked in a deep recession, with a crisis in the property market and unemployment running at 20%. In 2008, just prior to the economic crisis, Spain was constructing more houses than Germany, France and Italy combined. The Spanish housing bubble burst. Portugal saw its creditworthiness downgraded because the budget deficit for 2010 jumped to 9.3% instead of the anticipated 6.5%. In these circumstances, the current rate of the euro is simply too high for Greece, Spain and Portugal, but devaluation of the single currency is not an option. And so the only alternative is to slash government spending, with all the social distress and upheaval which this implies: demonstrations, strikes and political instability. In spite of all this, the danger of contagion is far from over and the entire Eurozone is at risk.

Many EU Member States are finding it increasingly difficult to form stable governments, since large sectors of the electorate are dissatisfied, and switch from one side of the political spectrum to the other, simply as a way of expressing their discontent. Political impasses of this kind quickly lead to economic stagnation – and it is this monetary instability, in particular, which strikes at the very heart of European integration. The two big European questions during the next ten years are: who pays the pensions and what is going to happen to the euro?

In 1995, Bernard Connolly – a senior monetary official in the European Commission – wrote a book entitled *The Rotten Heart of Europe*. His book sketched a scenario where the euro might one day fail because of the strains imposed by the widely differing economies within the European Union. He was sacked on the spot. Shortly before his death in 2006, the American economist Milton Friedman predicted exactly the same thing, citing 2015 as the likely year for the collapse. Europe tried to dismiss Friedman's arguments as the speculation of a hard-headed, asocial capitalist, someone who could not possible understand the ideological dimension of the *ever closer Union*. But as the year 2015 approaches, our monetary problems are getting ever bigger. Perhaps we should have listened to Friedman and Connolly after all? Perhaps we should – but listening is not the strong point of the European bureaucracy.

Yet while the mandarins carry on as usual, the peoples of Europe are starting to become worried. What does the *ever closer Union* have to say about these disconcerting matters? Not very much. Anyone who tries to raise these thorny problems in the European Parliament is instantly regarded as an idiot or a troublemaker. You can almost see members of the 'pro-European majority' shaking their heads in disbelief. The possibility of global marginalisation simply never enters their minds, since it is not compatible with their world vision of irreversible unification. Marginalisation is impossible! Europe is growing, its creation story has only just begun! However, this imaginary dream of the European elite, based on their Euro-centric mindset, simply does not square with the real facts of the situation. And unfortunately for them, facts are still more potent than self-deception.

But this is precisely the problem with the philosophy of the *ever closer Union*: it encourages an attitude of denial and leads to the development of illusory policy initiatives. Not even the European politicians can deny that our population is ageing, but many of them see immigration as the perfect answer to this problem. This is very, very questionable. Many West European countries combine a liberal social welfare system with a liberal immigration policy. This is a perfect combination to attract immigrants, but it also offers them a perfect reason to avoid economic integration, leading in turn to social and cultural isolation in ever-expanding inner city ghettos. Europe's problems are not being solved in this manner; they are simply being recycled and repackaged. And the European politicians, with the Socialists in the lead, approach this problem almost exclusively from the 'social question' of the previous century, without ever developing a perspective that is more appropriate to the current one.

The process of irreversible unification means that Europe's politicians – at least the believers amongst them – are psychologically ill-equipped to deal with this subject. Even the most carefully balanced posing of the immigration question is immediately dismissed as being 'racist'. To be honest, I sympathize with immigrants. As a journalist, I travelled extensively through Africa; a continent with few prospects in spite of fifty years of development cooperation. Many African countries are ruled by elites sponging off ordinary citizens. One of the biggest landowners of Brazil is the President of Angola. African elites store their capital in Swiss bank accounts, while their populations live in poverty. Had I been born in Nigeria, Ghana or the Ivory Coast, I would also try to get to Europe. But if millions of Africans cross the Mediterranean there is a problem; for Europe and for the immigrants, many of whom will lead the life of a pariah, shunned by Europeans. The only winners are the human traffickers impudently profiting from a failing European immigration policy. So, inconvenient questions have to be asked. But some of the questioners are immediately threatened with anti-discrimination procedures!

The EU is trying to develop an equitable immigration policy, but there is a huge imbalance between the admission of immigrants – which is fully in accordance with all the most politically correct theories of human rights – and the total absence of an effective system of returning those who seek to enter the EU illegally because 'procedures' are failing. Article 8.4 of the 2008 Return Directive states that involuntary return should only be used as 'a last resort' and that the necessary force used by the authorities must be 'proportionate to the situation' and must remain 'within reasonable limits'. These somewhat wishy-washy definitions have led to all kinds of legal test cases and increasing legal uncertainty. Illegal aliens are continually citing new information or new precedents, and the legal profession is quick to support them. In practice, tens of thousands of immigrants arrive in Europe illegally, but after a year of two of delaying tactics, most of their cases are 'regularised' – and they are allowed to stay, albeit in poor conditions. These new citizens then fan out across Europe, in the name of the solidarity of the nations preached by the *ever closer Union*. In 2005, Spain regularised the residence of more than 700,000 illegal immigrants, following which an almost never-ending stream of 'boat people' decided to risk the perilous crossing from the North African coast. An immigration policy without an effective return procedure is simply an 'open-door' policy. As a result, Europe continues to attract a tidal wave of displaced people whom it is neither able to accommodate nor absorb. Most of them are destined to live in the margins of European society, while human traffickers will be able to attract even more victims on the African continent. Unfortunately, Europe is not an open concept of freedom and opportunity which newcomers can sign up to. Instead, its societies are reserved, if not resistant to outsiders even from different parts of Europe, let alone to immigrants from other continents. There is no Statue of Liberty awaiting them.

European bureaucracy is not solving the continent's problems, but is simply helping to spread them. And most members in the European Parliament blindly close their eyes to the tensions which can be created by the different social and cultural perceptions of the newcomers. This is a taboo theme, which is very definitely not for discussion. In the name of multiculturalism, all moral and ethical values are declared to be equal. As a result, the old continent is losing its identity and its cultural self-confidence. What Europe really needs is a cultural revival, but instead the European elite is locked in a process of cultural capitulation. This serves to create a sense of inner frustration amongst their population and voters, of which the recent Swiss ban on minarets is a clear reflection.

With regard to the plight of the euro, the *ever closer Union* has no other remedy than to continually adjust its criteria to the latest round of out-of-control budget deficits. Initially, the Economic and Monetary Union had clear criteria, which included a maximum budget deficit of 3% and a national debt equivalent to no more than 60% of the Gross Domestic Product. At the time, it was said that these criteria were 'written on tablets of stone'. Some of the smaller lands failed to meet the required norms and were issued with letters of warning by the European Commission. Like naughty schoolboys, they were told that they 'must try harder'. However, when France and Germany both ran up budget deficits in excess of 3% – and this in a favourable economic climate – the EU decided that it was time to change the rules. Now the offenders were encouraged to return to the 3% limit 'in due course' – and so the process of eroding the monetary union was begun. If Germany and France can ignore the 3% rule, thought the Greeks, then why can't we? And so they did – big time.

As we enter the second decade of the millennium, most of the countries in the Euro-zone are unable to meet the old criteria: everywhere deficits are growing and national debts are rising. Nobody was wise enough to save during the 'good years', and so the price is being well and truly paid now that the 'lean years' have arrived. Moreover, it is doubly difficult to reduce state deficits in most EU countries, since the state is usually a major employer. In Europe, the public sector, protected by powerful trade unions, is untouchable. They consistently resist reform, pushing their countries into bigger debts. For a number of years, Greece actually published fake figures for the level of their budget deficit, but even then they were forced to admit that it amounted to a massive 7%. In reality, the true figure was a mind-boggling 13%. The European Commission knew for quite some time that the figures had been doctored, but decided to say nothing. The Commission thought: if they kept quiet, surely things would get better, wouldn't they? No, they wouldn't. The Commission clearly failed in one of its core tasks.

However, in some respects this ostrich-like policy is forced upon them. In theory, it is not possible to oblige a country to leave the Euro-zone. The Treaty of Lisbon does contain a global exit-procedure, which was designed to act as a kind of veiled threat to those countries whose Euro-critical populations continued to say 'no' in their referenda. This would allow Brussels to threaten 'expulsion' from the Union *tout court*, no doubt with hell and eternal damnation as a further consequence. But there is no such exit procedure for the Euro-zone. This would potentially be more useful (and necessary), but once again it is incompatible with the belief that the *ever closer Union* is irreversible, although there is already a visible crack in the Eurozone. In fact, two Euro zones are emerging: *l'euro d'olive* and *l'euro du beurre*.

The common currency can only work if its highest principle is the fiscal solidity of its Member States. For too long, the states were allowed to finance a policy of public waste and inefficiency because fines to punish the fiscal rule-breakers do not work. So, Greece thought it could have its cake and eat it. Now the Euro-zone members – read the German government – have only come to rescue Greece in a 'last resort operation', involving the IMF. German taxpayers are not willing to bail-out Greek profligacy and in case of a looming default the Greek government will have to go 'cap in hand' to the IMF headquarters in Washington DC, like Great Britain did in 1976. The monetary squabbles about the euro demonstrate convincingly that the *ever closer Union* is an ill-conceived concept, if not an illusion, because the words *ever* and *closer* ran into their limits. The West Germans generously agreed to finance their fellow countrymen in East Germany with hundreds of billions of euros. The Germans are, though grudgingly, the biggest contributor to the EU budget. But Germany is really overstretched if it has to bail out other European countries. Europe cannot always presume the Germans will pay. That is precisely where the *ever closer Union* closes. Greece has shown the limit and the Eurozone is running into the buffers.

Is there an alternative to the federalism of the *ever closer Union* or are the Europeans doomed to follow their chosen path to destruction?

In this book, I will attempt to break the monopoly over the European creation story currently claimed by the protagonists of the *ever closer Union*. Their orthodoxy needs to be rigorously tested and challenged, because it does not work. They are simply slowing down the rate of our decline, rather than doing anything fundamental to reverse it. In short, they are driving the peoples of Europe to revolt against the European ideal. The peoples feel less and less sympathy with the European institutions, because these institutions are paying less and less attention to the matters that really concern them. Everywhere I go in Europe, it is clear that local people and local politicians regard the question of immigration as a 'problem'. Everywhere, that is, except in the ivory towers of Brussels. The European elite speak with great circumspection about this key issue, for fear of offending anyone. It is political correctness gone mad.

The European Parliament is the place where this new debate must be conducted. There needs to be a confrontation between the accepted European wisdom and other, alternative ideas. That is how a democracy is supposed to work. The Plenary Chamber must become the birthplace for a new vision of the European future – a vision which I call the *United Europe of*

States. Not the European elite, but a new Europe of Peoples must provide the inspiration which will allow us to halt our downward spiral, bringing an end to economic stagnation, a failing pensions system, a damaged currency and a cultural capitulation which goes against everything Europe stands for. This concept of a United Europe of States is much closer to ordinary Europeans of every nationality than the current consensus in the European Parliament in favour of the irreversibility of the unification process. The psychological framework for citizens in Europe is their nation state; Europe is only united when its Member States agree, either by unanimity or qualified majority, on issues where they share sovereignty. The concept of the *ever closer Union* has reached its boundaries, because the Member States of that Union are no longer willing to be absorbed further into a European state, let alone their citizens. Supporters of that concept deny that this boundary exists and continue to press forward. But it exists – and right behind it lies the fault line that could split Europe apart. There is a French saying: *chasser le naturel, il revient au gallop.* Flying in the face of the facts is courting disaster. That is precisely what the European Parliament is currently doing.

2

THE EVER CLOSER UNION

If water forms the true divide between nations, then the English Channel should really be the size of the Atlantic Ocean. There is no greater difference in 'European vision' than between the Belgians and the British. The relative positions of the two countries are indeed oceans apart, a fact I have often been forced to confront as a Dutchman elected in Belgium (Flanders), but as a member of a political group in the European Parliament which is largely dominated by the British Conservatives.

The Belgians and the British have completely different emotions whenever anyone mentions the word 'Europe'. For the Belgians, Europe is the answer to all the problems that they are unable to solve in their own country. For the British, the European Union is a kind of necessary evil, a reserve position forced upon them after the fall of the British Empire, the mightiest empire the world has ever seen. Emotionally, many Brits are still attached to this empire which no longer exists. It was a multi-culinary empire whose menu contained the very finest dishes selected from Africa, Asia and the Caribbean. No wonder that they are disappointed, now that they are once again confined to their own island and with nothing better to look forward to than a daily diet of fish and chips! The heart of the British still rests far outside Europe: only their mind is in it – and this for purely pragmatic reasons. They are in Europe because they have to be in Europe, because there is nowhere else to go, because it is the 'rational' choice. But they still speak of the *United Kingdom* and *Continental Europe*, as though these two geographical entities belong on different planets.

On 24 February 2010, the British anti-European MEP Nigel Farage launched a fierce, full-frontal attack on the President of the European Council, Herman Van Rompuy. Farage – who is in favour of the UK withdrawing from the EU – ranted and raved at Van Rompuy in a manner worthy of the very best British football hooligan. British politicians are usually well-mannered, but Farage is a real street-fighter. In the European Parliament, he compared Van Rompuy to a 'damp rag' who had all the charisma of a 'low-grade bank clerk' – although he failed to specify precisely what is wrong with being a low-grade bank clerk. To round it all off, he called Belgium – Van Rompuy's country – 'a non-nation'. The President of the European Council looked shock and puzzled, as though this tirade couldn't possibly be meant for him. You could see him thinking: 'How can an MEP possibly be so anti-European?' Slanging matches of this kind are also quite common in the Belgian Parliament, but there no one takes them seriously. But for a Belgian, 'Europe' is of a much higher order.

Belgian politicians speak of Europe in a curious mixture of poetry and prose. Even the most cynical of Belgian ex-premiers get a visionary gleam in their eyes once they arrive on the European scene. Wilfred Martens, Leo Tindemans, Jean-Luc Dehaene, Guy Verhofstadt, and now Herman Van Rompuy: they are all EU-driven. They all want to do in Europe what they were unable to achieve in Belgium. They want to rule at a higher level, freed from the parochial atmosphere of the village fete and the local cycle race, which somehow seems to typify domestic politics in their native land. After thirty years or more of provincial Flemish patriotism, they see Europe as their new *Heimat*, a place of boundless idealism, where they can forget the endless bickering between the Dutch-speaking Flemings and their French-speaking compatriots. Europe is their golden *fin de carrière*.

In comparison, British politicians – at least the more civilised ones – show a kind of lofty detachment towards Europe, and hide their criticism of its institutions in typical British 'understatement', so as not to shock their European colleagues. But they have no real affinity for the European Union, and absolutely none at all for the 'European conviction'. In their eyes, the European Union continues to be a 'bastard' organisation, which of course can in no way be compared to the late, lamented British Empire – the empire which, according to them, brought 'culture' and 'civilisation' to the entire world. After the decline and fall of the Empire, geography and economics determined that the British future – like it or not – lay somewhere in Europe. If a British prime minister talks about the European Union in Westminster, he usually does so with frequent reference to 'British interests'. He speaks of 'red lines' beyond which he and his government will not go. Every commitment given in Brussels is weighed against a national interest which needs to be defended at home. This is true irrespective of the political colour of the premier and his party. He can not tap the endless fountain of 'Euro-love' which is available to his Belgian counterpart. If he did, he would be branded a Europhile. Viewed from a British perspective, it is no surprise that this term of political abuse rhymes with the word paedophile. In fact, a paedophile would probably get a better hearing from the British electorate. During election campaigns, every political candidate studiously avoids the word 'Europe' for fear of the negative emotions it will arouse. British MEPs are almost permanently banished to Strasbourg until the elections are over, and if they are allowed back into the country before polling day, they are told very firmly by their party whips: "For God's sake, don't mention Europe!"

The different emotional responses of the Belgians and the British towards Europe can be easily explained. Great Britain is an 'old' nation with a very well-defined identity. This identity mixes with the European identity slightly less well than oil mixes with water. As the focal point of its own empire, Great Britain was Europe's greatest-ever global power. The British horizon was not Europe, but the world. The British held the European continent at arm's length and their most important political objective was to prevent the formation of a European coalition against their island stronghold. Nor was this just a question of Anglo-Saxon paranoia. On two occasions, Europe did indeed unite and very nearly overthrew the Empire: first under Napoleon, later under Hitler. Somehow, the British never really took Napoleon all that seriously: after all, in their eyes, he was just a midget Frenchman, with all that the term implies, who quite properly met his Waterloo at… Waterloo. It was a different matter with Hitler. If you go into a British bookstore and look for the section marked 'Germany', you might be forgiven for thinking that the country ceased to exist following its defeat

– largely by the Russians, of course – in 1945. Almost all the books are about the war. Books about the subsequent Federal Republic are almost non-existent. And the Battle of Britain continues to define the British mental attitude, even today. British literature, British television and British humour are still full of figures such as Captain Mainwaring, Herr Flick of the Gestapo and Basil Fawlty shouting 'don't mention the war' in front of his German guests. A united continent has always been a danger to Great Britain, and for many British people – and certainly for many politicians – it still is. The British therefore persist with their time-honoured policy of 'divide and rule', breaking up coalitions, or forming coalitions of their own which will create enmity rather than unity. For example, London is still Europe's largest financial centre, but the British will do anything to stop Brussels from getting its grubby little hands around the neck of the chicken – The City – that still lays the golden British egg. Not that the British are alone in this. The French would react in a similar fashion if the subsidies to their farmers came under threat, and the Germans if the future of Volkswagen was at risk. But the British reaction is always that little bit more extreme. From the left to the right of the political spectrum, they all seem to think that the European will succeed where the *Luftwaffe* failed: in breaking the British economy.

A fixation with the European balance of power has therefore been a constant feature of British foreign policy for centuries. A 'disunited' Europe maximised their chances for the realisation of their expansion plans elsewhere in the world. If the

Channel was safe, their island was safe. Little wonder, then, that the modern concept of a 'united Europe' still evokes different feelings amongst the Brits when compared with the reaction of most continental Europeans. The Empire has long gone and the British economic focus is now clearly on Europe, but the old historical reflex is hard to avoid.

The European Union's internal market certainly provided the British with a useful alternative to their lost colonial markets, and for this reason they are prepared to accept the 'common market' as the basis for the process of European economic integration. But they still get nervous once other themes start to be mentioned. The idea of the 'ever closer Union' still causes hackles to be raised in London and has Downing Street reaching for the section of the European handbook marked 'opt outs'. They are the eternal European 'outsiders', who will only be dragged kicking and screaming towards greater political integration.

Belgium's position in Europe is very different, both historically and politically. The regions that now comprise modern-day Belgium were successively fought over and occupied by the Spanish, the Austrians, the French, the Dutch and the Germans (twice). When the Belgians finally managed to secure their independence from the Kingdom of the Netherlands in 1830 – a process know in Belgium as a 'revolution' and in Holland as a 'revolt' – it was very much a late-comer on the European stage. The country was created because the British wished to prevent either the French or the Germans from getting their hands on the port of Antwerp and the estuary of the River Schelde: if the Channel is safe, our island is safe. As a result, London pushed forward King Leopold I, – a member of the Saxe-Coburg family – whose late first wife Charlotte would have become Queen of England had she lived, who himself had just missed out on being chosen for the Greek throne, and was now prepared to chance his arm in Brussels. In other words, the British 'creation' of Belgium was not an act of charity but a calculated act of power politics.

Belgium was now a state, but it was not a nation. In fact, some Flemish politicians have even called their country's genesis 'an historic mistake', or at best 'an accident of history'. In order to try and generate some kind of national sentiment, King Leopold II decided to follow the British 'colonial' approach. His eye fell onto Congo, a rich land in the dark heart of Africa, which he came to regard as his personal property and which he exploited in a manner bordering on the shameful. As the decades passed, Belgium gradually underwent a socio-economic transformation, with the Walloon provinces becoming poorer – as a result of the decline of their coal and steel industries – while the Flemish provinces became richer, particularly after the Second World War, thanks largely to foreign investment. Linked to this economic process, there was also a political process that sought to achieve the 'emancipation' of Flanders within Belgium, a theme that is still alive today.

Belgium sits geographically at the heart of Western Europe, and for this reason has always been one of the continent's great transit lands, like Poland in the east. People have always been coming and going, or simply passing through. Often these were traders. Sometimes they were armies. The First World War, fought on Flanders Fields, not only caused huge loss of life but also serious economic damage. Twenty years later, the Second World War saddled the nation with a political time bomb. Part of the ruling elite, including King Leopold III, had tried to come to an agreement with Hitler. After the war, this resulted in a souring of domestic relations between different regions and different parties, and led to a desire to settle old scores. King Leopold III – who even visited Hitler in Germany – lost his throne, while the thousands of Flemish militants who had thrown in their lot with the Nazis were deprived of their civil and political rights, if not their lives. Leading collaborators fled abroad – the Walloon Leon Degrelle sought exile in Spain, while the Flemish socialist Hendrik De Man was accidentally killed in Switzerland in 1953 – but this tended to camouflage the fact that most sections of the cultural political elite had attempted to reach some kind of accommodation with the occupying authorities.

Given this divided and divisive situation, the idea of European unification came as a gift from heaven for the Belgian post-war political establishment. In many ways, it was an almost existential solution. European unification meant that Belgium would no longer be a battleground for foreign armies. Instead, Belgium would become the economic gateway to Europe. Geography – which had caused the country so much misery in the past – would now be the source of its salvation. With Brussels as its capital, Belgium now sat at the very centre of the continent – or at least its western half. Little wonder that Belgian politicians and diplomats were at the forefront of this unification process, or that Belgian schoolchildren were taught that Europe was 'the answer' and that they must grow up to become 'good Europeans'. For Belgium, Europe was an *Ersatznation*.

But there was also a second reason why Europe seemed to solve so many of Belgium's problems. As the tension between the Dutch- and French-speaking communities continued to rise, from 1970 onwards successive Belgian governments embarked on a process of state reform. By 1966, Flanders had overtaken Wallonia as the nation's economic motor, and this led to a corresponding shift in the political balance of power towards the Dutch-speaking north of the country. As a result, the Walloon politicians were now prepared to concede increased political autonomy to Flanders, in return for Flemish subsidies to prop up the ailing coal and steel industries in the south. This transfer of competences away from central government and towards the regions has now been going on for four decades, and is still not complete. As a consequence, the political agenda during this period has been characterised by 'less Belgium' and 'more Flanders'. This political battle is not only a matter of language and rights – although these are currently very visible on the surface – but mainly a question of cold, hard cash. With the very real prospect that the Belgian State might soon disintegrate, the concept of European integration seemed like a very useful port in a storm. 'Europe' became a substitute for a 'Belgium' that had never really existed as a nation. A 'united Europe' would provide the answer to the questions that kept the Flemish and the French-speakers divided. Do you want a useful piece of advice? Never ask a Belgian about his identity, unless you have a couple of hours to spare. You will be treated to a long and complex story about villages, regions, countries and continents, and at the end of it you will probably be none the wiser. Belgium has Dutch-speaking Flemings, French-speaking Walloons, a French–speaking Brussels bourgeoisie, native 'Brusselaers' (who are supposed to be Dutch-speaking), French-speakers living in Flemish villages around Brussels and a small enclave of German-speakers who are usually lumped together with the Walloons, but get along well with the Flemings. Brussels, the capital of Europe, Belgium and Flanders alike, is at the heart of all this and equally a bone of contention. Belgian national sentiment is no longer able to unify these diverse regional groupings, and so Europe must do what Belgium cannot. In short, as Belgium unravels, its identity is being gradually absorbed into a European identity. Most Belgians are not worried by this; they probably couldn't care less. The fact that the first President of Europe is a Belgian therefore has a dual symbolic significance: the last outburst of Belgian national pride and the first step – if not a giant leap – along the road to national emasculation.

Belgium's pro-European sentiment must therefore be viewed against the background of a very specific national situation. It offers a way out to a society and a political system that is very close to grinding to a halt. This is why nearly all Belgian politicians are in favour of 'more Europe', almost irrespective of content. They are in favour of a European government, with European taxation and a European army. Try getting that through the Houses of Parliament! But the Belgians have absolutely no problem with any of these concepts.

This, of course, helps to explain why the Belgians and the British so often seem to collide within the European Union. The Brits see Belgium as some kind of geo-political joke, whereas Belgian diplomats are resolutely 'anti-British'. These tensions often come to the surface, and are not necessarily the result of the actions of a one-man political kamikaze squad like Nigel Farage. For example, in 1994 Germany and France both put forward the Belgian premier Jean-Luc Dehaene as a candidate for the presidency of the European Commission. However, the Dehaene candidacy was blocked by a veto from Prime Minister John Major at a European summit meeting in Corfu. Major wanted to show his supporters back home that he had the same 'backbone' as his predecessor, Margaret Thatcher, and that he would not accept a pro-European federalist at the helm of the most important political body in the EU. As a result, the job went to the Luxembourg premier, Jacques Santer, whose opinions did not differ all that widely from Dehaene's, but who had a less outspoken profile.

In 2004 it was Guy Verhofstadt – another outspokenly pro-European prime minister – who wanted to become chairman of the European Commission. He argued openly in favour of all the things the British hate: taxation at a European level, greater political integration, a European army, etc. Not surprisingly, he became an instant target for the British premier Tony Blair, who persuaded a number of other government leaders to block the Verhofstadt bid.

And finally, in 2009, there came yet another Belgian prime minister to give it a try: this time for the 'Presidency of Europe', no less. Herman Van Rompuy succeeded where Dehaene and Verhofstadt had failed: he managed to avoid the British veto. In part, this was due to his own tactical skill – Van Rompuy is a cynical but smart politician. However, the biggest factor working in his favour was his almost total anonymity in European circles. Moreover, he had a degree of political insight that Verhofstadt had never possessed. This allowed him to conduct a low-key campaign, emphasising his willingness to serve. The fact that he had never expressed radical federalist opinions in the past also worked in his favour. He cultivated the image of a blank page, on which Europe could write its own manifesto – and so he was able to persuade even the British premier, Gordon Brown, to keep his veto in his pocket.

The government leaders of the major EU member states tend to see Van Rompuy as some kind of faithful errand boy or even – dare one say it – low-grade bank clerk, but they would be unwise to underestimate him. In contrast to many other politicians, he has the ability to link tactics and strategy and he is an expert in backstairs negotiation. As chairman of the Christian-Democrat CVP party, he has had plenty of experience at political intrigue and wheeler-dealing. In 2003, I sometimes used to have breakfast with him at the headquarters of the Flemish Christian Democrats. Over coffee and croissants, he explained to me how he had seized power in his party and how he had been forced to carpet several of his leading colleagues for their extra-marital indiscretions. 'Do what you like, but in God's name, do it in private!' On these occasions, he showed a mixture of humour and cynicism that I had not seen before. He is astute, sharp and devious, perhaps even a bit vicious.

Back in those days, the Liberal Party of Premier Verhofstadt tried to paint a picture of Van Rompuy as an old-fashioned Catholic traditionalist, yesterday's man from a bygone generation. An 'old crocodile', as they liked to term it. They wanted to create a spectre of an ultra-conservative Van Rompuy, who was determined to destroy Verhofstadt's regime of enlightened free-thinkers. The Liberal leader once talked of "that scrawny little scarecrow who came to measure my office". Some on the centre-left even tried to claim that he was a member of Opus Dei. This is a rumour that I can scotch. During that period I attended a number of Opus Dei meetings for a book I was writing, but never once did I come across Van Rompuy in secret conclave with the agents of Rome. In reality, he is a cultural conservative, but he is sufficiently flexible to do political business with everyone. Notwithstanding all the machinations of Verhofstadt, Van Rompuy was able to make one of the few successful political comebacks in Belgian politics. Against all odds, he was appointed Speaker of the Federal Parliament in Brussels since the provinciality of the Flemish Regional Parliament doesn't really interest him – he leaves that to his brother, Eric, and his son, Peter. Against even greater odds – and much to everyone's surprise – he then went on to become Prime Minister of Belgium, and then President of Europe. Van Rompuy is proof of the fact that there can be life after political death, and he now has the job (oh, irony!) that Verhofstadt would have so dearly loved. During Verhofstadt's animated pro-European speech at Van Rompuy's first visit to the Strasbourg Parliament, I paid particular attention to the new President's facial expression. Here was the man who had once called him "that scrawny little scarecrow" now singing his praises to the world. I am sure that I detected a certain quiet satisfaction in his restrained grin, as though this was a moment of historical atonement. Finally, Europe has its own cardinal-president, or rather its *cardinal gris* , who has more up his sleeve than Nigel Farage could ever imagine. Europe is now his vocation, and the circle of government leaders is his curia.

Belgian politicians have always been fervent prophets of a federal Europe in their own country and they support the European elite in Brussels in their 'European conviction'. But in this respect, Belgium is still the exception rather than the rule in Europe as a whole. In terms of mental perspective, the average European citizen is still the citizen of a nation state. The British regard themselves as British, the French as French, etc. The elite in the Wetstraat and the Berlaymont Building think, or rather hope, that these nation states will gradually fade away, or at least be eroded, but this misguided belief is the biggest single mistake they make. The nation state still has plenty of life left in it, and will continue to form our political frame of reference for generations to come.

After the recent extension of the European Union with a further twelve Member States, the federal ideal has become completely unobtainable. The new Member States arrive in Brussels looking to express and secure the interests of their own nations. Forty years ago very few of them were free. The Baltic States didn't even exist, but were simply provinces of the greater Soviet empire. Given recent European history, it must be obvious to anyone with eyes in his head that the nation state is the starting point for the formation of public opinion in just about every European country. Unsurprisingly, that is not the view of the mandarins in Brussels nor of the European Parliament in Strasbourg, both self-proclaimed guardians of unlimited unification. They are divorced from public opinion and move in an imaginary world of their own making, the ivory towers of Europe.

In 1988, the British premier Margaret Thatcher gave a speech at the College of Europe in Bruges. This college trains the Eurocrats of the future, and so from the Iron Lady's point of view she was walking into the lion's den. Nevertheless, the speech has gone down in history as one of the most anti-European addresses in history. But if you now re-read the text some 20 years later, it is difficult to see what all the fuss was about.

She said: "Let me be clear. Great Britain does not dream of a cosy, isolated existence on the fringes of the European Community. Our destiny is in Europe, as a part of that Community.

But this does not mean that our existence is solely determined by Europe. But this applies equally to France, Spain or many other countries."

In 2010 there are few Europeans – Frenchmen and Spaniards included – who would argue with this statement.

She went on. "The Community is not a goal in itself. Nor is it an institutional framework which needs constantly to be adjusted in accordance with the dictates of some abstract intellectual concept. Similarly, it must not have as its objective the proliferation of legislation. The European Community is a practical way for Europe to ensure its prosperity and the safety of its peoples, in a world filled with other powerful lands."

In other words, the European construction is not the be-all and end-all of everything. It is a means to an end, not the end in itself. Once again, few people – outside Brussels – would quarrel with this today.

She then came to the part of the speech that caused the greatest commotion: "My guiding principle is this: a willing and active cooperation between independent, sovereign states is the best guarantee for a successful European Commission. The attempt to suppress the nation state and to concentrate power in the hands of a European conglomerate would be very damaging and will endanger our final objectives. Europe is much stronger because France is France, Spain is Spain and Great Britain is Great Britain, each with its own traditions, customs and identities. It would be madness to try and force them into some kind of European entity."

A British prime minister – of whatever party – could still comfortably express these same sentiments today. But so too could a prime minister in Spain, Poland or the Czech Republic. No French president would ever dream of allowing his nation to be squeezed into 'some kind of European entity'. On the contrary, he is more likely to see Europe as an extension of France, and to demand a leading role for his country. And this is exactly what President Sarkozy is doing. Similarly, the heads of state in Lithuania, Hungary, Estonia, and so on see Europe as a stage on which to express their national ambitions within a safe context. They, too, have no intention of being absorbed into a European identity. They didn't fight for forty years to free themselves from the yoke of communism, only to submit tamely to European centralism.

As we enter the second decade of the new millennium, Margaret Thatcher is a hero in America, an icon for the Russians, and a liberator for the newly independent states of Eastern Europe. But in Brussels her name is seldom mentioned. She is the anti-Christ. The European Parliament is full of halls and rooms dedicated to the great politicians of the last half century: Adenauer, Spaak, Brandt and Spinelli, who was the founding father of the European Constitution. There is even a Petra Kelly Room in honour of the memory of the standard bearer of the German Green movement. But a Margaret Thatcher Room is unthinkable. No majority in the European Parliament would ever vote for it.

Even if I were to mention her name during an ordinary debate, it is certain to be greeted with catcalls and jeers. It was she, for example, to the great annoyance of many, who forced through a reduction in agricultural subsidies at the European summit in Fontainebleau in 1984, where she demonstratively demanded her 'money back'. At that time, the agricultural policy was swallowing up some 65% of the European budget; now it is down to less than 45%. Some see this as a feather in her cap, since it freed funding for other important policy areas, such as research and development. This was all Thatcher's doing, but her name is still not to be spoken in polite European circles. The very mention of the T-word is enough to give the European federalists the jitters.

Prime Minister Thatcher's fears, expressed in Bruges, have now all come true. When she made her speech back in 1988, Europe was just emerging from a period of Euro-sclerosis. During the economic crisis at the beginning of the 1980s, the European Community seemed powerless to help, but the new President of the European Commission, Jacques Delors, was able to give new propulsion to the European project with his plans for the completion of the internal market. Moreover, the European Community had just completed the implementation of the European Act, which gave enhanced powers to the European Parliament. There was a general feeling that Europe was riding the crest of a wave, a feeling enhanced by a strong recovery in economic growth.

The great 'European' event in modern history occurred just a year later: the fall of the Berlin Wall. Suddenly, the whole perspective was changed and the European Community took a giant leap forwards with the Treaty of Maastricht, which laid the foundations for political and monetary union. The Community changed its name and became a Union – an 'ever closer Union'. This expression had been part of the European Treaties from the outset but after the fall of the Berlin Wall, it seemed to get a historical boost in the Maastricht Treaty. But again, European citizens were hesitant. The French voters nearly rejected Maastricht in a referendum, while the Danes needed to go to the polls twice before a 'yes' vote could be obtained. Brussels might have taken a giant leap forward, but it was clear that large sections of the European population were not leaping with them. After Maastricht, the gap between the mandarins and the people grew ever larger, since the European elite simply assumed that the 'ever closer Union' would be a process of unification without end.

In short, the process had become 'irreversible'. The Treaty of Maastricht was followed by the Treaty of Amsterdam, which gave yet more powers to the European Parliament. This in turn was followed by the Treaty of Nice in 2000, which gave the Union 'the green light' to enlarge into Central and Eastern Europe. This time it was the Irish who needed to go twice to the ballot box before they could be persuaded to say 'yes'. And so the tempo of enlargement continued to gather pace. As Thatcher had warned, the nature of the European construction had indeed become an end in itself. The ink on the Treaty of Nice was scarcely dry before the next judicial draft was rolled forward. This was the so-called Declaration of Laken, which proclaimed that the next step in the unification process was the formulation of a European Constitution! A Constitutional Convention was quickly thrown together, made up from representatives of the European elites in the Member States, and they produced a draft that was signed by all the national heads of state in Rome, just two years later, on 29 October 2004. The momentum of the 'ever closer Union' seemed unstoppable and irreversible.

Until, that is, the public got involved once more. Most European citizens had probably lost track of the quick succession of European treaties and declarations, but occasionally they were required to go to the polls to express their opinion. The French President Jacques Chirac had promised a referendum on the constitution, believing he would win it comfortably, whilst at the same time further dividing the French socialists, his domestic political rivals. The Netherlands also decided to hold a referendum – for the first time in its history. In both countries – founder members of the original Community and both perceived as pro-European – the vote was a resounding 'no'. In order to prevent this trickle of resistance from turning into a tidal wave, the ratification process was temporarily suspended and instead a period of reflection was suggested. Not that this was really necessary. The people of Europe had already made their opinion clear: they did not want a European Constitution! Most of them had their own national constitutions, which they found perfectly adequate. After much soul-searching and debate, the Union was eventually able to save part of the constitution by re-drafting it into the Treaty of Lisbon. This time, however, the government leaders were careful to avoid promising their national electorates a referendum on the ratification process. The exception was Ireland, which again needed two ballots to achieve the desired result. It is hardly an edifying example of democracy in action. In America, the guiding political principle might well be 'We, the people', but in Europe it is more a question of 'We, the peoples.'

And so history has proven Maggie Thatcher to be right, after all. The people of Europe have made clear that they are not interested in a supra-national federal structure, into which they must be 'absorbed'. Europeans share a centuries-old European culture, with common Judaic-Christian roots, but they most definitely do not share a common European identity. In this sense, the European Constitution was misleading. From 2000 to 2010, the European Union became so wrapped up in the process of its own institutional reform that it forgot to give a say to the people who really matter: the citizens of Europe. And these citizens, in whose name these sweeping reforms were carried out, had few means, if any, of restraining the runaway enthusiasm of the European institutional elite. The European Parliament simply continued on its merry way, irrespective of turn-out and results, and the people were simply told to keep on voting until they finally voted 'yes'.

This is very different from the situation in America, where the electors have the opportunity to send a signal to the new president soon after he has taken office. This is what happened to Barack Obama, who was elected by a comfortable margin in 2008, but misjudged the mandate that the voters had given him. His victory in terms of electoral college votes was impressive, but the overall popular vote was just 53% for Obama and 47% for his Republican rival, John McCain. Hardly a crushing majority, and one which suggested that a middle-of-the-road policy might be advisable for the early months of his presidency. Instead Obama proceeded to implement a left-of-centre programme that was based largely on the agenda of the ideological leftist fringe and the trade unions within his own Democratic Party. State debt shot through the roof and the budget deficit soon reached record levels, largely because the new president had pumped too much money into his attempts to aid the financial sector, stimulate the economy, save the motor industry (at the request of General Motors) and introduce an expensive system of universal health insurance. President Obama made the biggest leap from the freedom ideal, of which the US is the guardian, to a European style equality ideal since President Franklin Delano Roosevelt's new deal in the 1930s.

Many Americans began to get the impression that Obama was trying to change the very nature of America by transforming the economy from a largely private-funded enterprise into an economy largely dictated by government intervention. Some critics even claimed that he was trying to 'socialise' Uncle Sam, 'socialism' being a dirty word to almost every American. There were fears that he would turn the USA into 'Euro-America', with a permanent budget deficit, a high national debt and even higher rates of taxation. In other words, Obama repeated all the mistakes Europe had made by pursuing 'socialistic policies'. It seemed, in short, as if he was flying in the face of the cultural-political perception of most ordinary Americans, for whom a deal of suspicion about the intentions of big government is built into their DNA.

Within a year, the electorate sent out a signal that they were not happy about this 'semi-European' course. The Democrats lost the elections for the governorships in New Jersey and Virginia. In January 2010, the results in the mid-term elections in Massachusetts – so often a Democratic stronghold – were even worse. The senator's seat which had been held for so long by the legendary Edward Kennedy was won by the Republican Scott Brown. This was a very clear shot across the bows, which warned Obama that he needed to shift his policy back towards the centre, if he wished to avoid a major defeat in the Congressional elections of November 2010. In short, voters were warning the President that in a period of just 12 months he had lost the credit that he had built up during the electoral campaign of 2008. It is now up to the President to decide whether he heeds this warning by adjusting his programme.

The Americans do have a correction mechanism to restrain their political elite. But what can the Europeans do in similar circumstances? Following the experiences of recent years, referendums are now studiously avoided, and the Treaty of Lisbon has its own self-amending mechanisms. The boycotting of elections to the European Parliament also does little to change matters, because this can be interpreted by the politicians as a form of silent consent. And even if the voters came to the polls *en masse*, for whom would they actually vote? The ideological concept of the 'ever closer Union' draws its support from all sides of the political spectrum: Liberals, Socialists, Christian Democrats and Greens. It doesn't leave a lot of alternatives. True, there are a few brave voices of protest, crying in the wilderness of the European Parliament, but their numbers are laughably small, and they are soon told politely but firmly to button their lips.

The European Union therefore has no effective correction mechanism for the 500 million people it purports to represent. The members of the European Commission are nominated by their member governments, usually as a reward for political services rendered, or because they have fouled their political nest in their own country. The President of the European Council is appointed by the national heads of state. This system is based on co-option – a system popular in that bastion of democracy, the Peoples Republic of China. The American concept of the 'correcting voter' is seen as a danger. "Correcting? What needs to be corrected?" In the European Union, the institutional elite always knows best. It borders on sheer political and intellectual arrogance similar to the infamous remark of Douglas Jay, a former British Labour Party politician, who wrote in his book The Socialist Case (1937): 'The gentleman in Whitehall really does know better what is good for people than the people know themselves'. Today, Brussels knows best. There is no alarm-bell procedure; no emergency stop button. This explains how Europe's politicians could be so engrossed with their own institutional reform that they failed to notice that the world outside Brussels and Strasbourg was undergoing fundamental change. It was political navel-gazing of the worst kind.

The world is not standing still. With this thought at the back of its minds, the European Union draws up a new strategy every ten years, full of ambitious targets. In 2000, the European Council launched the Lisbon Process. This was designed to ensure that Europe would become the most competitive part of the world, based on a level of technological innovation even greater than that of America. In official jargon, this was formulated as: "The European Union will become the most dynamic and competitive, knowledge-based economy in the world by 2010." Back in 2000, the atmosphere was euphoric. The Lisbon Process was written to reflect the circumstances of the 1990s: rapid economic growth, new global markets, the liberalisation of utility sectors, major technological breakthroughs, particularly in telecommunications. Europe would become a leading economic power in the new decade, with 3% of its GDP devoted to technological research and 12% to renewable energy.

The new century would be Europe's century, just like the 20th century before it. Why should the Union be cautious? Surely it was right to be positive, to set ambitious targets? It was less important whether or not these targets could actually be achieved. Intentions were more important than results. And just as well, since the results certainly failed to match up to the targets set. In 2007, the 27 member states of the European Union were spending an average of just 1.8% of their GDP on research and development. Performance for renewable energy was also below par. Of the 20 best universities in the world, 15 are in the USA and 5 in Great Britain. In 2009, there were just two French universities in the top 40. Germany, which less than a century ago was a pioneering nation in the field of technical education, was nowhere to be seen. The best German educational institution – the Munich Technical University – occupied a lowly fifty-fifth place. The spirit of Van Humboldt is long dead, and the European knowledge economy seems to be finding it hard to get off the ground.

If we take the awarding of Nobel Prizes in the exact sciences as another indicator, the situation does not get much better. Since 1990, 115 Nobel Prizes have been awarded to the United States, with just 49 going to Member States of the European Union. Great Britain heads the European list with 19 Nobel awards, followed by Germany with 13, France with 7, and the Netherlands and Hungary, both with three. And with each passing decade, the Americans are strengthening their position in relation to their European rivals.

How can this poor showing be explained? To a large extent, it is the result of two very specific mistakes which the European Union keeps making time after time.

1. Gesture politics. Instead of making hard choices and hard decisions, the EU prefers to kick at an open door. By opting for easy policies, everyone agrees – simply because there is nothing to disagree with. Brussels wants to create a perception of unity, an image of harmony that does not reflect

the realities of the situation. In 2006, the European Commission took the decision to try and reduce the Union's technological shortfall in comparison with the United States. With this aim in mind, a European Institute of Technology (EIT) was founded, which was intended to rival America's Massachusetts Institute of Technology (MIT), one of the top ten universities in the world. But in 2010, the EIT – located in Budapest – is still nothing more than a symbol, disguised as an EU agency. Four years after it was launched by the European Commission, it is not really operational. It was intended that the Institute would prepare and propose a strategic innovation plan by the end of 2011, but tangible results are still beyond reach. In other words, the EIT is no rival at all to the illustrious MIT. Even so, the EIT proposal was well-received when it was first put forward back in 2006. It made for some encouraging headlines. At last, Europe was 'doing something'. But what exactly was Europe doing? No one bothered to ask and EIT soon dropped off the public agenda. The EU could make a much more serious contribution towards innovation if it took effective measures to create a community patent, since this would ensure that Europe's inventors could protect the legal rights to their intellectual work at relatively low cost. Many of them now move to the United States, where this type of uniform, cheap, easy and enforceable system is already in operation. Largely for this reason, Europe has lost almost its entire pharmaceutical industry research and development infrastructure to the Americans.

Not only was much valuable knowledge lost in this manner, but also the opportunity for a significant number of high-quality jobs. It is still difficult to acquire a patent in Europe, with its patchwork quilt of Member States, and the administrative and translation costs are prohibitive. A proposal for a European patent actually does exist, but it is currently being blocked by a judicial problem with the Germans, and a political problem with Spain, which insists that Spanish must be used alongside English and French as a standard language for the documentation. And what is good for the Spanish must also be good for the Poles, or the Greeks, or the Italians, and so the Union finds itself back where it started: precisely nowhere. The project just sits gathering dust in a Brussels drawer, like it has done for the past ten years. The European Union simply ignores this kind of core problem and takes refuge in gesture politics. But if nothing is done about the patents problem, the European brain drain will continue, much to the benefit of the US and India. And there are dozens of other dossiers where much the same is true.

2. Setting unrealistic objectives. The European Union forms objectives that bear no relation to reality – and are therefore wholly unattainable. Instead of adjusting its targets and setting its sights a little lower, it reacts by setting even more ambitious objectives. This is simply a question of going from bad to worse. The 12% GDP target for renewable energy was not achieved. So how does Europe react? By set-

ting a new target of 20% by 2020, which is even more unrealistic. In December 2009, the European Council decided that by 2020 the EU must cut its carbon emissions by 20%, in comparison with the 1990 figures. But under 'favourable circumstances' (i.e., if the other developed lands also play their part), this target would actually be increased to 30%. This was before the failure of the climate conference in Copenhagen. As a result of this fiasco, the 30% figure is virtually impossible and even the 20% target must be in doubt. But how does the European Parliament respond? By sticking stubbornly to its 30% objective, almost as if the stalemate in Copenhagen had never happened. It is almost like a poker game, where the players keep making higher and higher bets – until their bluff is called. But if anyone suggests that this policy might be short-sighted, even dangerous, they are soon shouted down. This, say the European believers, simply clouds the issue and casts doubt on the ideal. Once again, intention is everything, results are nothing. The word 'ambition' has therefore become synonymous in Europe with collective self-deception. By the same token, 'realism' is simply a sign of 'lack of conviction'.

The objective of making good Europe's economic deficit with America by 2010 was another pie-in-the sky scheme. In the 2000-2008 timeframe, the average growth of the EU economy was 1.7 percent whereas the US economy increased by 2.2 percent. In the same period, EU labour productivity increased by 1 percent, America's by 2 percent. In September 2008, the US and the EU were struck by economic and financial near-meltdown. Europe is currently in a deeper crisis than the US, and will probably take longer to get back onto its business feet. Anno 2010, what is the picture? The US recovers fast, the EU lingers on. Therefore, many European plans sound pretentious even before they have failed. They are reminiscent of some of the Soviet claims from the era of the planned economy. At the end of the 1950s, the Russian leader Nikita Khrushchev visited the United States. He saw full shelves in all the shops and he asked his American hosts to explain the secret of their success. "Maize", he was told. And indeed, American agricultural production is to a large extent based on maize. After a visit to the Maize Belt in Iowa, Khrushchev was convinced. When he got back to Moscow, he decided that he would also base the Soviet common agricultural policy on maize – or 'koekoeroeza', as it more poetically sounds in Russian. He convinced his Politburo comrades that 'koekoeroeza' would lead them to a golden future, and the propaganda department was soon devising a plan to convince the peasants, based on the slogan, albeit somewhat unusual for a communist regime: "Maize, the Tsarina of the fields!" Posters showed calves and cows grown fat on maize, promising increased production of milk, butter and meat. In short, the Garden of Eden recreated on the bleak Russian steppes.

Of course, nothing of the kind happened. Maize is ideal for feeding cattle, but not for feeding people. Grain production plummeted and the Russians soon found themselves faced with a serious bread shortage. In his initial enthusiasm,

Khrushchev had promised that the USSR would overtake the USA in maize production by 1980. Instead, large sections of the population were facing empty shelves and long queues. Nikita's Garden of Eden was full of the sound of rumbling stomachs. He began to complain that maize was obviously a 'capitalist crop', since it refused to flourish in the rich socialist earth of Russia and the Ukraine! However, he had no option but to try and do something about the empty plates and the empty bellies; and so the Soviets were humiliatingly forced to import grain – from the USA! Khrushchev was finally forced out of office in 1964, but many old Russians still say 'koekoeroeza' whenever his name is mentioned!

This story might be Russian, but it could just as easily happen in the European Union anno 2010. With its penchant for unrealistic objectives and gesture policies, the EU is conducting its own modern-day version of 'koekoeroeza' politics. As with the Soviet Politburo, the European elite is free to dream up its own far-fetched ideas, safe in the knowledge that there is little that the people can do to stop them. And if things go wrong, it will be the people who will be faced with empty plates and empty bellies – or in the EU's case, greater unemployment, higher taxes and increasing poverty. But the patience of the European citizen – like that of the Russian peasant – is not limitless.

This is a major problem, since Europe is rapidly approaching its decade of truth. Where will the European Union be in fifteen years time? Will it still even exist? Gradual economic and demographic declines seem to be heralding in a process of permanent erosion and decay. This can only be halted by effective entrepreneurship, economic innovation at an operational level, and easy access to risk capital. The message coming from Brussels must be clear and unequivocal. But is it?

The European Union has now launched its EU 2020 Programme, as the successor to the Lisbon Process. In contrast to Lisbon, EU 2020 does at least sound a note of urgency. If Europe continues to fall behind in the decade ahead, it says, the results could be catastrophic. But this message needs to be framed more dramatically and more bluntly, if it is to penetrate into the spirit of the people. However, this is not the EU's strong point. The European Commission, as an institutional arbitrator, has always had the tendency to try and reconcile everyone and everything under the soothing blanket of its political prose. In its original working document, the Commission wrote: "The objective of EU 2020 is a sustainable social market economy, smarter and greener." In the document presented to the European Parliament and the European Council the term 'market economy' was scrapped, and there was mention instead of "a strategy for smart, sustainable and inclusive growth."

But what does this mean exactly? How can Europe sharpen its competitive position and lead the way in technological innovation? Microsoft, Apple, Google and Pfizer are not European corporations. At the same time, Europe is losing industrial capacity hand over fist, and the labour market is leaking jobs at an alarming rate. If Brussels continues to push through its ambitious 2020 environmental objectives – without China and the US making similar efforts – the European chemical industry will be dead in the water before 2020 ever arrives. In Belgium, 94,000 people currently work in the chemical sector, a third of them in the Antwerp region alone. Antwerp has the world's largest concentration of chemical factories, after Houston, Texas. The sector also provides another 150,000 indirect jobs. In other words, some 250,000 Belgians earn their daily bread from the chemical industry. There has recently, and rightly, been a major commotion about the loss of 3,000 jobs with the planned closure of the Opel car plant, also in Antwerp. But the collapse of the chemical industry would be 83 times worse! What will the mandarins in Brussels say to the tens of thousands of new jobless if employment opportunities are throttled by an 'ambitious' climate policy? Stuff happens?

EU 2020 recognises the threat posed by 'demographic challenges'. Hallelujah! But what is Europe going to do about it? The labour participation rate for men and women must be increased from 69% to 75% and the social system must be modernised, so that there is an affordable answer to society's future needs. How? According to the Commission: "This means that the new policy must contribute in a demonstrable manner towards greater social cohesion, the fight against unemployment and the protection of social inclusion, whilst at the same time encouraging the labour market to improve its levels of performance." OK, but how? Is this a policy statement or a game of European hocus-pocus for advanced players? The EU credo is: 'Smart growth, sustainable growth, inclusive growth'. It sounds a bit like "great weather, clean air, lots of holidays". It is motherhood and apple pie. Nobody is going to disagree – it is yet another example of kicking at an open door.

What is the average European citizen to make of all this? It is striking that EU 2020 hardly mentions China, India or America in its text, while it is certain that the economic balance of power will inexorably swing towards these countries during the next ten years. Europe is still thinking eurocentrically, even though it is threatened with marginalisation to the fringes of the world economy, possibly to a degree much worse than the Icelandic volcano could ever achieve.

There is, of course, one truth which nobody is prepared to admit, and this explains why the term 'market economy' disappeared from the original European Commission draft. In an economy based on a common currency like the euro, devaluation is not a real option, because the underlying economies of the different member states vary too widely (cf. Germany and Greece, for example). Some countries would benefit from devaluation (Greece, Spain, Portugal, Italy) but others like Germany or the Netherlands would not, because they adhere to price stability and a stable common currency. This means that there is little room for a macro-economic policy and for 'demand economy', an economic stimulation plan in keeping with Keynsian theory. This is a recipe for budget deficits and massive levels of state debt, which will eventually undermine the value of the common currency. This is something that we have already seen. Monetary union has meant that an improvement of the economic situation can only be achieved via micro-economic policies: companies must become more competitive, taxes reduced and the size of the public sector limited. This is not the 'demand economy' (the state stimulating demand by higher government expenditure) but rather a 'supply-side economy': companies innovating and producing at competitive prices in the world market. It is not Keynes who offers the right economic theory for a common currency zone: it is Schumpeter, Von Hayek or Von Mises. You can take your pick from any of these three Austrians, but it all comes down to the same thing. And Milton Friedman – whose parents also emigrated from the Austro-Hungarian Empire – is their worthy successor! There is a compelling, economic logic: competitive companies resulting from low fiscal burden lead to limited government. The state sector needs to slim down, in order to make room for the competitive and innovative private sector. But this is hardly compatible with the maintenance of an extensive welfare state network, which in most (West) European countries is rapidly becoming unaffordable. This message – and its unpalatable consequences – is not a popular one with voters. And this is the elephant in the room that the writers of EU 2020 dare not mention. What is their answer? Bye-bye market economy! This is why the Commission retreated to the safer verbal territory of 'smart, sustainable and inclusive'. But is this smart? Is it sustainable? In the long run, is it inclusive? If it is to be so, the money will have to be earned in the European private sector. The EU is currently creating a mismatch. It tends to pursue the equality ideal by embracing a demand economy, accepting a higher level of taxation, overregulation and big government, whereas genuine recovery can only be created by way of the freedom ideal: enhanced competitiveness through increased innovation, which requires lower taxes, access to venture capital and limited government. The EU tries to reap the juicy fruits of the freedom ideal by implementing the methods of equality thinking. And that does not work.

EU 2020 proposes that 3% of national GDP should be reserved for research and development. The Lisbon strategy also contained the same objective, but it was not achieved, bottoming out at just 1.8%. As an alternative, why do EU Member States not agree on a zero level of corporation tax for all company profits ploughed back into R&D? Or propose similar arrangements for innovative SMEs? The ultimate consequence of the euro is that it forces Europe to become a supply-side economy. Perhaps it might be useful to send the members of the European Commission and the European Parliament a few books written by the above mentioned Austrian trio. In a competitive world economy, the government spending theories of Keynes – so highly praised in the corridors of Brussels – are simply tearing the Euro-zone apart.

For the mythical and hard-pressed European citizen, the year 2020 will probably be a question of 'make or break'. Will the economy still be growing, will there still be work, will the pensions still be paid, will the euro still be holding its own? What is our agenda for survival in a world where Europe is no longer its focal point? The President of the Commission increasingly has the appearance of a village priest, who is struggling to keep his congregation happy by trying to be all things to all men. He encourages the faithful, praises them for their belief and turns a blind eye to their failures. He is seldom angry or vengeful. He displays all the qualities of Catholicism, which, perhaps, is only right and proper in an organisation founded by the Treaty of Rome. But where is the logical, well-constructed and intellectually consistent agenda for European survival? Where will Europe be in 2020, at the end of a decade which promises a major demographic and geo-economic shift? Even the very question is frightening.

3
THE EVER BIGGER BUREAUCRACY

The European Parliament honours dissidents from around the world, but when at the beginning of 2009 the Czech President, Vaclav Klaus, aired his dissident opinions about Europe in the Plenary Chamber in Strasbourg, many of the assembled MEPs began to get a little hot under the collar. Some of them almost looked as though they had been slapped in the face.

Klaus was a guest speaker, and he made criticism of the European Union in general and the European Parliament in particular. This kind of behaviour was unheard of (certainly from an honoured guest!). Several of the Belgian members, federalists in heart and soul, left the chamber in near tears, and poured out their hearts in dismay to the waiting press. How was this possible? The President of an EU member state attacking the process of European integration! How dare he? Who did he think he was?

Government leaders and dignitaries from all over the world often come to address the Parliament in Strasbourg in formal sitting. And most of the government leaders of the member states – or at least very senior representatives – are also present to hear them. In November 2004, the South African President, Thabo Mbeki, spoke to the Chamber. He praised Europe and he praised the European Parliament. This was hardly unexpected, since the EU is one of the biggest aid donors to South Africa. As the speech progressed, Mbeki took as his theme the revival of Africa. He predicted a Renaissance. The parliamentarians bathed in the President's words of praise and listened fascinated to his story, without seeming to realise (or care) that Mbeki himself actually had very little to do with this revival.

In his own country, he was known for his somewhat unscientific views on the treatment of AIDS and his government actually hindered the sale of appropriate AIDS/HIV medication. While Mugabe in neighbouring Zimbabwe was plundering his land, in South Africa Mbeki did... almost nothing. He carried out what he called 'quiet diplomacy,' which was so quiet that Mugabe never even got wind of it. Instead of a Renaissance, Zimbabwe plunged deeper into Dante's Inferno. Mbeki just stood and watched.

Most of the assembled institutional Euro-elite seemed unaware of these realities, and just kept on listening to all the nice things he was saying about them. At the end, they first gave him warm applause, and then a standing ovation. He had offered them a little bit of jam, and they had lapped it up. For those who are susceptible to flattery – and which politician isn't – this was a feast of almost orgiastic proportions. They proclaimed Mbeki to be a "great leader", even though his own ruling ANC party had recently turned him out of office because of the ineffectiveness of his policies.

Klaus took exactly the opposite approach. Instead of coming to heap praise upon the European mandarins, he arrived looking for a genuine debate, and at least to speak his honest opinion. As president of his country, he is the leader of the Czech establishment, but by nature he is a rebel and he gave the European Parliament a kick in a place where they certainly weren't expecting it! During the Communist period in Czechoslovakia, he had been a dissident, and it was a habit that he had never grown out of. Unlike Mbeki, he had no major policy blunders to his name, but in Brussels he now ranks on a par with Margaret Thatcher. He gave his critical speech at the beginning of 2009, and afterwards, to make matters worse, he dragged his feet about ratifying the Treaty of Lisbon since he was the last head of state to sign. He was instantly labelled 'anti-European'. In the Berlaymont and the Louise Weiss Building, senior officials were almost afraid to mention his name, for fear of incurring the wrath of their political masters. He is the Voldermort of the European Union: the dark lord of evil whose name must never be spoken. But what did he actually say that was so terrible?

He called the European Parliament 'the key institution of the EU' (no problem there) and added that there was no alternative to the EU (and no problem there, either). But then it started. He said that the European Union must focus on four freedoms: the free movement of goods, services, persons and capital. Free markets always tend to silt up if there are too many legal obstacles. The removal of such obstacles was therefore a key task of the EU. The internal market is Europe's strongest card. He also added that Europe must find solutions for cross-border problems that individual countries were unable to solve.

The way not to do this, he argued, was to pursue too far-reaching a programme of integration which would create bureaucratic overstretch. He utterly rejected the Brussels gospel, which states that the <u>only</u> way forward for Europe is the 'ever closer Union', in other words a continuing progression towards ever deeper political integration, by which more and more nation states are absorbed into a single political entity. At the same time, he put the boot into the European Parliament. "In a normal parliamentary system, a part of that parliament supports the government and a part supports the opposition. This is not what happens in the European Parliament. Here, only one option is put forward, and everyone is expected to support it. Anyone who thinks differently is immediately labelled as 'an enemy of European integration'. Not long ago, we Czechs lived in a part of Europe where there was another political system that allowed no alternatives, and therefore no opposition. Our bitter experience of that system taught us that without opposition, there can be no freedom."

This was a stab right to the very heart of Europe's parliamentarians. A Belgian MEP later left the chamber in a rage, ranting that Klaus had compared the EU with the Soviet Union! But Klaus had never mentioned the Soviets. He simply pointed to the example of a parliament where no opposition was possible. But few of the MEPs were in a state to appreciate this fine distinction. Emotions were running high. They had been attacked in their own cathedral, and by a member of their own establishment! They were used to hearing this sort of nonsense from marginalised extremists, but from the President of a member state! Nothing like it had ever been seen before. And, of course, they immediately proved Klaus's prediction right, by branding him 'an enemy of Europe'. He now occupies pride of place in the gallery of European heretics, along with Mrs. Thatcher and a select group of others.

Yet amidst all the fuss, people lost sight of another telling point that Klaus had made. He said that within the current economic system the European Union was relying with increasing frequency on central planning. "Although history has clearly shown that this is not the right way, we are moving steadily in this direction." Klaus feared that Brussels would become a centre for micro-management on a European scale, which in turn threatened to develop into a form of social engineering, whereby Europe's policy-makers would attempt to determine human happiness from the comfort of their Brussels offices. The European elite believes that they know best how people can live in a 'happy and responsible manner', and are prepared to use legislation to 'persuade' the people of the logic of their arguments. What the citizens of Europe actually want for themselves is of no relevance. In fact, the less they know, the better.

Micro-management almost inevitably results in bureaucracy. In this respect, the European Union is by no means unique – as President Klaus would no doubt understand. The Soviet Union was another example of a major political-bureaucratic project, which theoretically had the best interests of the people at heart, but which tried to build this happiness on the twin pillars of micro-management and social engineering.

The Soviet Five Year Plans defined down to the very last detail the measures that were necessary for creating a 'state of human happiness'. In its heyday, the Soviet State Plan Bureau set something like 20 million prices each year. Of course, the Soviet Union and the DDR were extreme examples, and they were clearly sowing the seeds of their own long-term destruction. The unavoidable consequence of the state's rigidity was a growing divide between reality and rhetoric. Officially, their citizens were marching confidently towards 'a brighter future', based on the principle of human equality, whereas in reality they were stumbling reluctantly towards the edge of a precipice. And the faster the bureaucracy grew, the deeper the yawning chasm became.

Currently, many politicians want to replace the notion of Gross Domestic Product (GDP) with the newly invented expression Gross Domestic Happiness (GDH). The new term was immediately embraced by the People's Republic of North Korea, which called itself the leading GDH nation!

Bureaucrats who operate strongly from a centralised position in a top-down manner are paving the way for their own downfall. The human spirit – fortunately – is both elusive and intangible, and human behaviour can only be steered to a limited extent. The USSR and the DDR were classic examples of dirigisme, but similar mechanisms exist in every bureaucracy, irrespective of their objectives. Some of these objectives might even be 'noble' or 'well-meaning', but at the end of the day, it is the result that counts.

A good example of this phenomenon is the United Nations, an international organisation which fights poverty and organises peace-keeping missions – both of which are very noble objectives. But the UN is crippled by its bureaucratic structure, and its actions are at the mercy of its member states, in particular the five permanent members of the Security Council. The organisation serves a useful purpose as a forum in which all the nations of the world can come together, but in terms of pursuing its 'good causes' it is equally subject to the laws of bureaucratic inertia.

Much the same is true of the American Ministry of Defence, the Pentagon. Planning, procedures, hierarchies and competing human ambitions create an impenetrable forest of rules and regulations. The American army quickly won the war in Iraq, but its attempts to rebuild the shattered nation have been a disaster. The military bureaucrats were dropped into a country that they didn't know and they started improvising entirely on their own. Initially Iraq's cultural heritage was looted and then the country shifted into a state of civil war. Many lives were lost in vain because the military bureaucrats in Washington DC were insufficiently familiar with the realities on the ground. In the end, bureaucracies are usually forced to face reality because of the inherent impossibility of engineering their own people, let alone those of other countries. Human spirit and human ingenuity will always find a way to evade the imposition of rules from above. A bureaucracy that attempts to achieve too much – like the Americans in Iraq – will simply create chaos.

The European Union is no exception to this mechanism of bureaucratic overstretch, even though its objectives are also noble. European agricultural policy is a classic example. In reality, it is a form of planned economy, which in 2010 will consume 43.8% of the total EU budget. There is central price-fixing, and there are quotas and subsidies. The French call the Common Agricultural Policy (CAP) a brilliant success, because it ensures a guaranteed food supply and a reasonable income for (French) farmers. Most others see the CAP as a throwback to the Soviet era. In practice, most farmers are no longer entrepreneurs, but are semi-administrators subjected to the dirigisme of a state machine. The farming industry is tied up in Brussels' rules and regulations while the mortgage provisions are determined by the banks. Between the two, the poor old farmers can hardly move.

There is, moreover, a belief that agricultural subsidies only go to the farmers. This is simply not true – as became apparent in 2005 when the European Transparency Directive for the first time made it possible to publish the details of the end recipients of these subsidies. Many Member States tried to keep these details hidden for as long as possible, but the truth eventually emerged. And what did this show? Namely, that the lion's share of CAP subsidies found their way into the hands of huge multinational companies, such as Nestle, Tate & Lyle, Cargill, Campina, Greencore Group, etc. A number of Europe's major landowners – including more than one royal family – were also receiving EU funding. They get the biggest slices of the cake, and the farmers are left to pick up the crumbs. The agricultural industry is the real winner of Europe's agricultural planning mania – not the people who actually work the land.

Another source of European regulation that borders on micro-management and social engineering is the EU's environmental policy. Every European (even President Klaus) would agree that a European environmental policy is necessary. But few would share the enthusiasm of the Green movement for an 'environmental consumption quota' – through which the behaviour of people will be dictated by the needs of the environment.

In 2007, the Green Dutch politician Femke Halsema wrote that: "Environment is not just about morality. Environment is about people, about justice, about solidarity, about fair shares for all. An environmental consumption quota serves as a good example. We will really need to live our lives in a different manner."

This concept, which is based on the fairly unattractive idea that *people* = *pollution*, foresees that every man, woman and child will be allocated their own 'environmental consumption quota'. For example, if you take a holiday in Spain, you will not be allowed to take another one in the same year. Europe's citizens will not be permitted to fly or drive their cars 'too often' – a term to be defined by a new breed of environmental bureaucrats. The limits of what is 'permissible' mark the boundaries of the allocated 'environmental consumption quota'. Whoever has used up his quota for air travel or car miles, must use his bike, take a train – or simply stay at home.

This reflects a mania that many bureaucrats – and nearly all greens – have for attempting to socially engineer human behaviour. However, it is interesting to speculate whether this type of legislation would be applied to the MEPs themselves. If so, their quota would probably be used up before the first month was out, just with travelling between Brussels and Strasbourg alone! And all those study trips to exotic locations would have to go. The European Parliament might wish to impose 'environmental responsibility' on the peoples of Europe, but would they be equally strict with themselves?

The density of ecological regulation certainly smacks of central planning and statist dirigisme. At the end of 2009, the Dutch Prime Minister Jan-Peter Balkenende wrote a letter to Jose Manuel Barroso, the President of the European Commission. Balkenende asked him if it might not be possible to relax the European legislation relating to 'specially protected environmental zones', which together form the Natura 2000 network. Balkenende wanted to fight the financial and economic crisis in the Netherlands with a series of infrastructure projects on plots of land "ripe for building". However, Europe's environmental legislation is so precisely constructed that getting approval to build a road, dyke or bridge can take years. And it certainly does not allow for the kind of flexibility that Balkenende was seeking. Barroso sent him away with a flea in his ear. Brussels knows best. Brussels is boss.

Balkenende's major bone of contention was the Habitat Directive, which was adopted in 1992 during a Dutch EU Presidency. This Directive, which protects the habitats of 500 species of plant and 200 species of animal, was heralded at the time as 'an important step forward'. The Member States were even allowed to identify their own 'special protection zones' (SPZ) and the Dutch – no doubt wishing to set a good example

– rather overdid it. Large tracts of the Netherlands suddenly found themselves designated as an SPZ. Dozens of building projects were stopped overnight whenever a rare weed or an endangered insect were discovered on the work site. It is still the same today.

Groups of environmental activists roam the countryside like some kind of self-appointed Green police, assiduously searching out the habitat of the lesser spotted willow warbler or Thompson's long-eared bat. And when they find them, all further development – even on 'building-ripe land' – is shut down indefinitely.

In other words, even in times of crisis this Habitat legislation imposes a stranglehold on the freedom of national governments to stimulate their own economies. And if they try to create room for manoeuvre through a 'flexible' interpretation of the rules, there are always plenty of environment groups ready to take them to court, involving them in legal actions which can take years, if not decades, to resolve.

With its numerous NGOs (non-governmental organisations, many of them existing on European subsidies), the 'Green' lobby is by far the most powerful lobby in Brussels; far stronger than the agricultural lobby ever was. They set the agenda, launch campaigns in the press and do all in their power to ensure that the mass of environmental legislation is water-tight. Many MEPs are anxious to get into the good books of this powerful Green movement, and often accept their proposals without thinking twice. The support of the Greens wins them political capital with the voters, because 'green is good'.

This may just make all the difference between winning or losing their seats at the next election. Moreover, many MEPs have a Green background and a record of service with environmental action groups. Some of them behave like one-man NGOs.

Since there is no real countervailing power to the environmental lobby in Brussels, legislation is proliferating indiscriminately because all its policies have to be 'greened'. Greens create bureaucracy on steroids.

The Green movement, with Greenpeace in the vanguard, has conducted a long and intense campaign against Genetically Modified Organisms (GMO), as a result of which in recent years the European Commission has no longer allowed the development of GMOs, even though this is taking place throughout the rest of the world. The Greenpeace campaigns were based on scaremongering, which made GMO sound as though they were some kind of Frankenstein experiment for food. The European Commission was also slow to tackle the GMO question, since their approval fell within the jurisdiction of the DG Environment, which is generally regarded as the fifth column of the Green movement within the European bureaucratic system. During a meeting about GMO approval, attended by former European Commissioner Frits Bolkestein, the Commission President, Romano Prodi, once said: "Frankenstein food? It sounds almost as bad as Bolkestein food!" The President, like so many others, was clearly under the spell of Greenpeace.

Meetings about GMO were always difficult and ideologically charged. The result of this resistance was that the biotechnology industry in Europe could make little progress. The USA became the world leader in the biotechnology field, and snapped up the job opportunities that could otherwise have been created in Europe. But this is something that the Greens don't seem to care about: People are Pollution! In reality, their scaremongering about GMO is largely exaggerated. The development of yellow rice has made a significant contribution to the battle against hunger in Africa. This rice has been genetically geared to the specific growing conditions in that continent. In others words, GMOs can not only save jobs, but they can also save lives. During the most recent famine in Zimbabwe, the Americans sent food aid to help the hungry. President Mugabe promptly sent it back, because it contained GMO. He preferred to see his people starve.

But perhaps there are signs of improvement. In March 2010, for the first time in twelve years, the European Commission finally approved a GMO: a starch-rich potato. It hardly sounds like a major threat to world civilisation, but the Green group in the European Parliament was immediately up in arms. During the subsequent debate, they held up placards condemning GMOs in all their forms and the deputy leader of their fraction wept bitter tears of frustration at this 'sad day'. But the chance that they will ever find a GMO potato on their plate is non-existent. This particular potato is not intended for human consumption, but for the production of starch for the paper and textile industries. That, for Greenpeace, is beside the point. It is the principle of the matter that counts – and so they continue to be the NGO against GMO.

The aim of the Green lobby is to achieve a form of social engineering through greater micro-management in the European political-bureaucratic complex. Human behaviour must be regulated from Brussels, with directives, regulations, subsidies and sanctions. The Greens are not prepared to modify artificially what we eat, but they are prepared to modify artificially how we live. The wishes of the people must be subordinated to the needs of the environment, and Green NGOs continue to behave with a crusading verve that is seemingly beyond criticism, as in any religious belief system. The European politicians and media seem to be powerless in the face of this crusade. To attack a Green publically is almost equivalent to publically attacking a member of the royal family. Some critics, including President Klaus, see the Green movement as the 'new Red'. Like the old Soviet Plan Bureau, the thousands of Green NGOs in Brussels propagate rules, rules and more rules, without ever stopping to think about their effect.

For example, between 2009 and 2012 Europe will gradually impose a ban on the old-style incandescent light bulb. By September 2009, all the 100-watt bulbs had been withdrawn from circulation, to be followed by the 60-watt in 2011 and the 40-watt in 2012. This process was first started when the Green lobby was able to push through this ban in the Netherlands, with the support of Philips, the 'Mother of All Lamp-makers'. The production of the bulbs was no longer commercially interesting, and so in this instance good business sense seemed to coincide with the demands of the environmental movement. The measure passed with such ease through the Dutch Parliament that Brussels thought a Europe-wide ban must be a good idea. The European Commission made the proposal and the European Parliament approved it, almost without batting an eye.

And so the incandescent light bulb will disappear, along with the 3,000 jobs of the people in Poland and Hungary who make them. But this is a side-issue for the Green movement: once again, the needs of nature are more important than the needs of man. And how are we to see in the dark in future? The incandescent bulb has been replaced by the so-called energy-efficient bulb. This new generation of bulb does indeed use marginally less electricity, but they also produce a much dimmer light. To such an extent, that they are inadequate – and potentially dangerous – for many older people or people with impaired sight. Moreover, they also contain a highly toxic mercury vapour, which is anything but environmentally friendly! There are now plans to replace these new bulbs in the foreseeable future.

The banning of the old incandescent bulb was a pointless exercise, but to actually say so is 'anti-European'. Once a law has been passed by the EU, the only argument you hear is 'Europe says you must.'

During the debate on the incandescent bulb ban in the European Parliament, the Finnish Green politician Satu Hassi said: "This is an important step forward for the European Union. But it is essential that the bans should not be used as an instrument by irresponsible populists to arouse public resistance with incorrect information".

But in this instance, the incorrect information actually came from the Green movement itself. The Greens made a mistake about energy-efficient bulbs, and the European legislators meekly followed in their footsteps. But the ban, like so many other things in the EU, is irreversible, and so it now applies from Ireland to Italy and from Poland to Portugal.

The total package of European legislation amounts to some 90,000 pages, touching to a greater or lesser extent on almost every aspect of daily life. Public health, consumer affairs, environmental policy, company management, the financial sector, accountancy, taxation, tourism... You name it, and there is a European directive or regulation to cover it. Nearly every area of policy has been mapped and charted by Brussels. The few exceptions are asylum and immigration policy, financial oversight, legal and police cooperation between member states. But the mandarins also have plans to fill up these gaps in the near future.

In reality, what we really need is exactly the opposite: a giant 'clean-out' of the European legislative programme. This is easier said than done, because in a bureaucratic structure like the EU, every full stop and comma has its champion. Even so, the European Commission has recognised that the sheer weight of legislation risks becoming a source of criticism, and so they have now committed themselves to what they call 'better legislation'. Recently, they have even started to use the term 'smart legislation'. In essence, they have promised to go through the legislative package with a fine toothcomb. But will it ever happen?

In 2005, shortly after France and the Netherlands had rejected the European Constitution, the European Commission put forward a proposal to scrap 68 legal provisions, out of a total of 183 that it had investigated. In this way, the Commission wanted to create the impression that the EU's mania with rules and regulations was a thing of the past, and that the era of 'better legislation' had arrived. It seemed that the 'battle for perception' had been won. But appearances can be deceptive. A year later, only a handful of the provisions had been effectively deleted. In particular, the European Parliament was reluctant to see its work undone. There was always an MEP who could be found to say that this or that rule was 'vitally important'. Recently, the Commission proposed to reduce the administrative burden on business by 25% by 2012. This would save Europe's companies some 150 billion euros each year. It is the kind of thing that sounds great in the newspapers, but the task of sifting through the mass of relevant legislation is fraught with practical difficulties and objections. Each line of text has a bureaucrat, political constituency or an NGO who will defend it to the last. Scrapping regulations is the hardest task for any bureaucracy: it is almost like a form of self-mutilation.

Writing on this issue in the *Süddeutsche Zeitung* on 5 October 2006, Gunther Verheugen, a former vice-president of the Commission, said: "There are people who think that more legislation means more Europe. We must fight this image of Brussels as a bureaucratic monster. But not everyone in the Commission shares this objective." He made a similar plea during his farewell address to the Commission in 2010, but it will probably have little effect. There is no such thing as a legislator who doesn't legislate. The motto of every legislator is: 'I regulate, therefore I am.'

European legislation always has the tendency to go further and further, both in terms of scope and detail. Even the so-called process of 'simplification' allows Europe to extend its grip further. Combining two older pieces of legislation often creates opportunities for extending the scope of application and sharpening the criteria of the resulting new provision. Officially, there is talk of 'making things easier', but in reality the thumbscrews are being turned ever tighter. Extended scopes of application and sharpened criteria result in harmonisation in both breadth and depth.

This is a complaint that you often hear from the farmers, and the nature of their complaint is interesting. They bemoan a European environmental policy that leaves little room for agricultural enterprise. Farmers have been turned into 'agents' of the bureaucracy, implementing Brussels' policy through the mass of environmental rules to which they are subject. For example, many farmers are keen to sell their produce door-to-door, to escape from the cripplingly low prices offered by the supermarkets for their produce. But the labelling requirements imposed by Europe – even for selling a bottle of wine or a pot of jam to a passing tourist – are so stringent that the whole exercise becomes almost impossible.

Yet even the bureaucrats themselves are sometimes faced with similar problems. Some of the legislative packages that they have created are so large and so complex that they are actually difficult to implement. Take, for example, REACH, a provision which deals with the registration, evaluation, approval and limitation of chemical substances.

The provision was a problem child right from the start, and there were fierce debates in the European Commission during its decision-making process in 2003. The government leaders in France, Germany and Great Britain all phoned Commission President Prodi, asking him to bury the proposal. Prodi and his fellow commissioners wouldn't listen: chemical substances must be subject to registration and approval. Surely, they argued, that is a 'good cause'? Subsequently, the proposal was subject to more than 1,000 amendments in the European Parliament, and there was a major clash between the industrial lobby and the Green lobby.

Yet notwithstanding all these difficulties, the provision passed into law in 2006. As a result, the EU then set up the European Chemical Agency to implement its approval procedures. The agency was located in Helsinki, so that Finland could also have a European agency on its territory. It all seemed to be running smoothly – until the agency actually tried to perform its tasks. For example, the forward plan for 2009 foresaw the new registration of some 3,000-4,000 chemical substances.

But the actual number submitted amounted to 55,000! The exchange forum for information about chemical substances (SIEF) hardly functions, the agency is drowning in paper work and the chemical industry is losing money caused by the long delays in approving its new products.

In these circumstances, Brussels sees only one answer: more money and more bureaucrats for Helsinki. But in reality, the entire REACH programme is incapable of implementation. It is a result of micro-management gone mad, combined with the indifference of the European Parliament to the legislation it has already passed. Plans for new legislation are always much sexier and create media attention, but old legislation or detailed implementation? Who cares!

Whence does this passion for micro-management? Some people suspect the European Commission of being a bureaucratic conspiracy. Others see the European Parliament as being the guilty party, while the more paranoid believe that the President of the Commission has his own secret plan for world domination: they distrust him in the way that Protestants used to distrust the pope.

However, the pressure for greater micro-management is not the work of a conspiratorial mastermind, but is simply generated by the European political-bureaucratic complex itself. A bureaucracy produces rules: it is as simple as that. That is the nature of the beast. If there is no effective mechanism to hold the bureaucrats in check, the legislative process becomes self-perpetuating and gradually develops its own dynamic.

The process in the European Union is plain for all to see. The European Commission has a monopoly on the proposal of new legislation. Through the enlargement of the EU to 27 member states, the College of Commissioners has become much larger. Each country must have its own Commissioner, and so the College now has 27 members. Each Commissioner needs his own Directorate-General (DG) in order to make policy. The DG contains the collective knowledge that is necessary for preparing legislation. A Commissioner without a DG is like a general without an army. The number of Directorates-General has risen to 37, so that each Commissioner can be allocated at least one field of policy responsibility or even more. The increase in the number of Commissioners and DGs has also resulted in a corresponding 'balkanisation' of the administrative structure of the Commission.

In reality, about 18 Commissioners, supported by roughly 25 DGs, would be more than enough, but this is not acceptable for political reasons. As a consequence, the body responsible for producing Europe's legislation is dangerously top-heavy.

In particular, there are too many DGs and the division of policy responsibilities is not always consistent. The Barroso-2 Commission has many areas of overlap. There is a Commissioner for the Environment, but also a Commissioner for Climate Action. There is a Commissioner for Transport, but also for Maritime Affairs. There is a Commissioner for Development Cooperation, and another for Humanitarian Aid. There is one for Home Affairs dealing with immigration and one for Justice, who deals with cooperation between the police and judicial networks of the Member States. It is sometimes difficult to know to whom to turn first.

In addition to this enlarged College, in recent years the European Union has also set up no fewer than 37 separate agencies, many of which also have a clear legislative function. These European agencies range from: the European Food Safety Authority (located in Italy) and the previously mentioned European Chemical Agency (in Helsinki), to the more esoteric European Bureau for Fundamental Rights (Vienna) or the European Institute for Gender Equality (Lithuania). These 37 agencies are spread across the length and breadth of the Union and there are currently a number of new ones in the making, particularly in the financial sector, so that the total is soon set to rise above 40.

What is the consequence of this burgeoning number of DGs with overlapping competences in the College of Commissioners, supported by almost 40 agencies, acting as legislative outboard motors? The answer is simple. The consequence is more legislation, wider scopes of application and more specific criteria.

During the formation process for Barroso-2, candidate-Commissioner Michel Barnier went to his future DG and told them that he insisted on a new policy initiative at least once every two weeks. If all the European Commissioners did the same, this would mean 648 new policy initiatives each year!

The urge to legislate and micro-manage is built into the genes of every bureaucracy. Every DG wants to shine, every Commissioner wants an initiative to bear his or her name, no matter how trivial this initiative might be. A more structured setting of priorities and a greater degree of political direction could help to stem this legislative flow, but these things are sadly lacking within the European Commission. Each Commissioner puts forward his or her own proposals, and then refrains from criticising the proposals of his or her colleagues, in the hope that they will not criticise him or her. This tacit non-intervention pact means that everyone is allowed his (or her) place in the sun. 'Live and let live' seems to be the order of the day for Europe's policy-makers.

It goes without saying that everyone wants to get involved with the big prestige projects. A typical example is the Galileo Programme, which is intended to put Europe's own satellite navigation system in orbit around the earth. The initial proposal put forward by the Commission in November 2000 saw Galileo as a European equivalent to the American GPS system. There was nothing wrong with the US system; it was just that Europe wanted to have its own: 'more Europe', even in space!

I can still remember the meetings about Galileo, which I attended when I was working in the cabinet of Commissioner Bolkestein. The cabinet of President Prodi felt that Europe needed to be 'ambitious': Galileo had to shine as a genuine 'European project'. So, the Commission proposed 3.3 billion euros worth of ambition, two thirds of which was to be funded by the private sector. The aim was to have the system operational by 2007.

I was sceptical about the scheme and put a number of questions to my colleagues in the Prodi cabinet. Are we not underestimating the complexity of the project? Will we be able to find the private investors, in view of the fact that the American GPS-system is already up and running and being used by many European clients? Is the time frame realistic? How can we prevent costs getting out of hand? My queries were met with tuts of disapproval. I was suspected of being an 'unbeliever'. My comments were 'too negative'. I was told that we Europeans, like the Americans, needed to 'think big'.

The Prodi Commission had only just taken office, and was determined to use this prestige project to get their administration off the ground. When I suggested that it would be more likely to be a millstone around their necks – I think 'flying white elephant' was the term I used – I was politely thanked for my opinions in a manner which suggested that in future I would do better to keep my big mouth shut! The minutes of the meeting simply said that the Bolkestein cabinet had "made some minor observations". In this manner, our opposition was swept under the bureaucratic carpet. Case closed!

In 2009, the European Court of Auditors published a 'special report 9' on the Galileo Project which, as I had suspected right from the start, was turning out to be a nightmare. Bad management and technical problems had already caused a delay of five years. Private investors seemed uninterested in financing the project because there was no need for a European equivalent to the GPS-system. Costs had equally shot through the roof. Instead of 3.3 billion (already a colossal sum), the project would now cost an estimated 5.5 billion euros. Moreover, in view of the lack of private sector investment, this sum would now need to be financed by the EU, which means: national governments and ultimately the taxpayers.

The European Court of Auditors concluded that the original objectives were 'unrealistic', that the management of the project was 'inadequate' and that the funding arrangements had been 'badly planned'. The new target date for Galileo is now 2013 – if the money can be found. Most national governments are already faced with serious budget deficits, and the final price tag is still unknown.

In short, the EU had now got its 'white elephant', just as I had predicted – even if it is not yet flying! But of course, nobody is to blame. That is how the European political-bureaucratic complex works. It initiates a policy which may be a success or may turn out to be a catastrophic failure, but it is always the taxpayers of the Member States who are left to pick up the bill.

Even by European standards, Galileo was a derailed project, but the bureaucrats are also happy with smaller initiatives. These have the advantage of being able to slip through the Commission net almost unseen, but still result in the creation of additional legislation, which is the ultimate goal of every good bureaucrat. With the large, media-sensitive initiatives, it is usually the President and the Commissioners who run off with all the glory. You can hardly fit them all in the press photo! But it is precisely the unnoticed small schemes that lead to real micro-management. And with the increase in the number of Commissioners, DGs and agencies, there are always plenty of opportunities for schemes of this kind.

And once the schemes arrive in the European Parliament, the process is given a further push in that direction, since the parliamentary committees are all packed with MEPs who believe in 'more Europe' and who have actually fought for a place on a particular committee, so that they can promote their own ideals. So, the European Parliament magnifies bureaucratic overstretch.

In this way, for example, politicians who want 'more social policy' will have tried to secure themselves a place on the Employment and Social Affairs Committee. The Greens will try to wangle a place on the Environment Committee. Those who are concerned for the problems of the Third World will aim at the Development Committee. The farming lobby tries to pack the Agricultural Committee, while politicians from Europe's 'weaker regions' think that it may be useful to sit on the Regional Affairs Committee – and so on.

The most popular parliamentary committee is the Foreign Affairs Committee, with some 150 members. It is almost a mini-parliament in its own right! In contrast, the Budgetary Control Committee is less popular, with just 57 members. Why? The former involves lots of nice foreign travel; the latter involves the reading of lots of thick, stodgy reports. And besides: for most MEPs budgeting in any context is a relatively minor matter because the money will come through anyway. And what should we think of the Committee for Women's

Rights and Gender Equality? Around 95% of its 61 members are women – so not much gender equality there!

It doesn't require much imagination to guess the effect of this concentration of like-minded politicians in the parliamentary committees. In this manner, a parliament without opposition can actually become a cheer-leader for 'more Europe' – in other words, for more rules. Enthusiastic MEPs often find that the proposals of the Commission are not ambitious enough, and demand that they go further: stricter criteria, more intensive regulation.

They push for extra environmental and social impact studies, and often make 'own-initiative' reports, in which they ask the Commission to consider drafting specific legislation on a wide range of subjects, varying from the fight against obesity (which is indeed a serious problem in the European Parliament!), to gambling, the social economy, urban policy (isn't that a matter for local councils?), the regulation of venture capital and a policy for the 'avoidance of natural disasters', which unfortunately didn't do much to stop the Icelandic volcano paralyzing European air traffic. Europe feels that it has a right to regulate everything, even including volcanoes, earthquakes and tropical storms, though to no avail.

There is little thought for the unintentional consequences of these well-intentioned measures. For example, the EU issues a guideline on weekly working hours, but the result is a less flexible labour market and loss of jobs. France once introduced a 35-hour working week, in the hope that it would lead to more work for more people. The result was exactly the opposite, and it produced immediately a 10% rise in structural unemployment.

Yet lessons of this kind are never learned in the European Parliament. The Committee for Employment and Social Affairs demanded a limit on the working hours of self-employed lorry drivers. But this means that most of these drivers can no long run their businesses profitably. In other words, the EU organs responsible for creating employment are actually creating unemployment. In a similar vein, the Women's Rights Committee demanded five months' maternity leave, without seeming to realise that this significantly reduces a woman's chance of finding employment during her reproductive years, since few employers – in particular in SMEs – can afford to miss key staff for so long. So, the Women's Rights Committee produces unemployment for women!

This is not untypical. Many members of the European Parliament are so divorced from the economic realities of life in the everyday world that they seldom stop to think about the affordability of their noble plans. They keep passing one piece of social legislation after another. But this is exactly the reason why social measures should be left to the authority of the Member States – so that they can decide whether or not they are actually in a position to pay for them.

There must be a direct relationship between social rights and economic affordability. The standard of prosperity throughout the European Union is not uniform. Bulgaria cannot afford what Luxembourg can. Even so, the European socialists continue to push for a continent-wide minimum wage, which would leave a trail of economic ruin and unemployment in the newly entered Member States.

The 22 parliamentary committees of the European Parliament turn the mills of legislation into overdrive. The Parliament continually criticises the Commission for being too bureaucratic, but in reality is no better itself. But self-criticism is not Strasbourg's strong point. In fact, the Parliament bears a bigger share of responsibility for the EU's micro-management than the Commission, because it actually intensifies the mechanism. Its task is to assess the Commission's proposals critically, but all too often it simply rubber-stamps or even magnifies them. By nature, the Parliament is too often just a mutual congratulation society in the hope that proposals that an MEP wishes to promote will be free from criticism by colleagues. MEPs apply the same sort of non-intervention principle as European Commissioners do. Everybody wants to bathe in the same warm bath of consensus.

So, the European Parliament actually pushes the process a stage further: it wants to become a 'co-director' in the European project, establishing a *régime d'assemblée*. It wants to rule alongside the European Commission, so that it can have a more direct role in the steering and management of legislation. This would not be a good thing, since it would turn the Parliament into a part of the problem instead of keeping it as a part of the possible solution. Even though it doesn't do a very good job of it, Parliament is the only EU institution that can control and monitor what the Commission is doing.

But how could it control the Commission if it was also partly responsible for the Commission's failures? Parliaments that attempt to rule alongside their executives inevitably create crises.

Consider, for example, the case of the American Congress, which was responsible for setting the course of the two giants of the American mortgage market: Fannie Mae and Freddy Mac. These were both government-sponsored enterprises (GSEs) which pumped hundred of billions of dollars into the housing market each year. In total, America has something like 55 million mortgages, half of them with Fannie and Freddy, good for a total sum of five trillion dollars. This is equivalent to almost 50% of America's Gross Domestic Product. Members of Congress – whether Republican or Democrat – all see home ownership as an integral part of the American dream. This was reflected in the fact that in 2006 69% of Americans lived in their own homes.

To make this possible, Congress insisted that mortgages should also be offered to less well-off citizens, particularly to those in minority groups. The credit terms were lowered accordingly, and if this meant that Fannie and Freddy occasionally found themselves short of cash, they could always go and knock on Congress's door. And to make sure that things ran with a minimum of fuss and delay, Congress was also kind enough to ensure that supervision and regulation were kept to a minimum. But when the housing market collapsed, Fannie and Freddy suddenly found themselves hurtling towards bankruptcy. The house-owners were unable to pay off their loans, the banks folded and the stock market crashed, because share prices had been based on a mortgage boom which no longer existed.

In the preceding years, Fannie and Freddy had repeatedly frustrated the attempts of the American executive to guard against this eventuality, simply by appealing for help from their high-placed friends in Congress. And Fannie and Freddy treated their friends well. Very well indeed. Some of them were given 'sweetheart deals' for their own mortgages and several received campaign funding for their political activities. The third largest recipient of campaign funding by Freddy and Fannie was then-Senator Barack Obama. And, curiously enough, Fannie and Freddy building projects often seemed to be concentrated in the electoral districts of these friends. It was political incest of the worst kind.

However, by September 2008, both the mortgage giants stood on the verge of breakdown and the government put them into receivership. It was, however, too little too late, and within a week the whole financial sector was in meltdown. The origins of this crisis were, of course, many and complex, but it was the irresponsible practices of Fannie and Freddy that lit the fuse. And both were jointly run by Congress, which in the weeks following the crisis saw its credibility rating with the American public fall to an all-time low of 20%. It was an object lesson in a golden rule of state organisation: the parliament's task is to monitor and assist in the implementation of legislation. It is not its task to govern: that is the work of the executive. So, no *régime d'assemblée!* This rule should also apply to the European Parliament.

In the European Parliament, the pressure for detailed legislation is further stimulated by about 15,000 or so lobbyists – both companies and NGOs – who offer the parliamentarians ready-made amendments to the Commission's proposals. These interest groups often have very specific knowledge and seek to use the legislative process to secure their own position. In so doing, they are perfectly within their rights, but they inevitably feed the tendency toward over-regulation. As result, the bureaucratic mill moves up to turbo-speed!

It might be expected that the member states would try to stem this flow of rules and regulations, and block detailed legislation in their own national parliaments. But it is very seldom that a European directive is torpedoed during the course of its passage through the legislative process. Perhaps this is because European legislation also gives power to the very national bureaucracies which are charged with transforming European directives into national law.

The Habitat Directive is a good example. It gave the member states the authority to initiate their own 'special protection zones' (SPZ). The national Ministries of the Environment were obviously in favour of this procedure, since it meant that the zones in question would fall under an ecological regime for which the ministries themselves would be responsible. In other words, it extended their power. This meant that many national ministries tried to apply a very broad interpretation to the criteria of an SPZ, so that large tracts of land soon found themselves included within these zones, as Premier Balkenende later found out to his cost in the Netherlands. And because 'green is good', the EU decided to unite these extensive zones within the Natura 2000 network.

In other words, national environment officials were able to 'import' power from Brussels, so that their ministry and their minister could climb another rung on the domestic ladder of political influence. And much the same principle applies to other areas of policy, such as public health, monitoring of financial services, education, culture, tourism, regional development, consumer protection, immigration, employment policy and social affairs. European policy is also national domestic policy, since every policy has a European dimension. It's a bit like Catch 22.

Little wonder, then, that there is so little resistance to Brussels at national bureaucratic level. Domestic ministries can use the excuse of 'Europe says' to acquire competences that they would never be able to acquire in other circumstances. Effectively, they are partners in crime.

It is simply not in the interest of national ministers and their staff to oppose 'more Europe'. On the contrary, it allows them to tailor the legislation in their own countries more closely to their own requirements. The concentration of bureaucratic power in Brussels has never led to a corresponding reduction in national bureaucracies. The argument put forward by some Europhiles that the European bureaucracy will eventually replace these national bureaucracies is sheer nonsense.

The massive bureaucracy of the Common Agricultural Policy was never implemented at the expense of the national Ministries of Agriculture. On the contrary, these national ministries became more important than ever. The same is true of environmental policy: the more EU environment directives we have, the greater the power of the environment ministries in the member states will become. And always the arguments are the same: 'the intention of the legislation is good' and 'Europe says we must'.

The Belgian model proves conclusively that bureaucrats – whatever their origin – have a natural tendency to reproduce themselves. From 1970 onwards, Belgium gradually transformed itself into a federal state, which resulted in the systematic transfer of powers to the regions. You would think that this might lead to a reduction in the number of bureaucrats at the federal state level, working on the assumption that fewer responsibilities need fewer staff to carry them out. Not so.

In 2010, the University of Leuven published the results of a report commissioned by the National Government Institute. This showed that the number of Flemish civil servants had risen from 38,230 in 2000 to 45,249 in 2007, largely due to the development of semi-independent state companies, such as De Lijn, the regional bus service. However, during the same period the number of federal officials also rose by over 5,000, to reach a total of 83,871. In other words, competences are being transferred away from the central government in Brussels, but bureaucrats continue to flow in. The position was even worse in the Brussels Capital City Region, which received very few new competences, but where the number of officials increased by over 25%, to a new total of 6,911.

In short, bureaucracy is like the mythical hydra: you cut off one head, and two more grow in its place – certainly in Belgium, where the civil service is regarded as a kind of national job creation scheme: 17% of the Belgian workforce is now employed in a state-related function, the highest percentage in all Europe. The European Union needs to be careful that it does not go the same way.

Part of the problem is the question of duplication. The European Union performs a number of tasks that are already carried out elsewhere in Europe by non-EU organisations. For example, there is a Council of Europe in Strasbourg which operates far beyond the boundaries of the Union. Its 47 members include Russia, the Ukraine, Turkey and the republics in the Caucasus. Even so, the EU decided to set up its own European Agency for Fundamental Rights in Vienna, which does almost exactly the same as the Council of Europe in Strasbourg. Instead of leaving human rights matters to another perfectly competent organisation, the EU simply has to have its finger in every pie. And so it opts for duplication, in preference to simplification.

Basic democratic freedoms are adequately protected in all the European Union's member states. These freedoms are usually enshrined in the national constitution and the various common provisions of the different European treaties. However, the Treaty of Lisbon decided that something additional was required: namely a new Charter of Fundamental Rights. Furthermore, the Lisbon Treaty also forces the EU to accede to the European Convention for the Protection of Human Rights. Member states are invited to accept the European Court of Human Rights in Strasbourg as the ultimate arbiter in such matters.

This is typical of the way Europe works. Why is there a compulsion to build up different layers of rights? The chance that Europe will ever be confronted with a series of General Pinochet-like figures, determined to eradicate popular liberties, is fairly remote. Yet to guard against this vague possibility we now have three different levels of protection: the Treaty of Lisbon, the Charter of Fundamental Rights and the Convention for the Protection of Human Rights. Too much of a good thing, perhaps?

To make matters worse, this kind of proliferation inevitably leads to confusion, complications and clashes of interest. What are the respective powers of the European Court of Justice in Luxembourg and the European Court of Human Rights in Strasbourg? What are the respective positions of these courts with regard to the national courts in the member states? Some of the recent rulings by the Court of Human Rights have come very close to interference in domestic politics. For example, it recently judged that the display of crucifixes in Italian schools was in contravention of the constitutional separation of church and state. Most Italians (perhaps understandably) were inclined to think that this was none of Strasbourg's business – all the more so since the complaint was actually made by a Finnish lady! If she is so allergic to crucifixes, why did she go and live in Italy, a Catholic land where crucifixes are an integral part of the cultural tradition? But no, Europe wants to be all things to all men and women, and so the Finn must have her 'right' protected – even if it is at the expense of 59 million Italians, living in their own country.

In a similar vein, the Belgian Senator Jean-Jacques De Gucht suggested that crucifixes should be removed from Belgium's cemeteries. It seems that not even the dead are safe in Europe anymore. But should these really be matters for the EU to decide? If France wants to ban the burka, surely that is a question for French society as a whole and not just for the Court of Human Rights in Strasbourg? It cannot be the intention that Europe dictates to its Member States how they should arrange the internal organisation of their national way of life.

Accession of the EU to the Convention for the Protection of Human Rights is a good example of a bad 'good' idea. No one would dispute that human rights need to protected, but the manner in which the principle is implemented allows the EU to penetrate into almost every aspect of private and national life. The Treaty of Lisbon states that the Convention "enshrines the general principles of the legislation of the Union".

This means that notwithstanding the Court of Human Rights' backlog of some 100,000 cases, it has generated a substantial body of jurisprudence that will automatically migrate to the EU *acquis*. In this manner, the EU will be given access to policy areas – religious symbols, family law, education, culture, labour relations – which properly belong under the jurisdiction of the nation states. The ink of the Court of Human Rights' ruling on Italian crucifixes had not dried before the European Parliament started drafting urgent resolutions to address the issue. That is the way in which the European political-bureaucratic complex imports new powers through the backdoor.

The European Parliament often has the pretention to claim that it is the manifestation of the sovereign will of the 'citizens of Europe', but several national legal institutions are starting to question this perception. For example, in a pronouncement made on 20 June 2009, the German Constitutional Court (*Bundesverfassungsgericht*) argued that the European Parliament cannot be considered to be truly representative, since its members are not elected on the principle of one man-one vote. This means that larger member states have relatively few MEPs, whereas smaller member states have relative more. The figures vary between 96 for the largest country (Germany) and 6 for the smallest countries (Luxembourg).

As a result, Germany is under-represented and Luxembourg over-represented. 'Against this background, the European Parliament remains, by virtue of the quota of seats allocated to the member states, simply an institution representative of the peoples of Europe'. The German court then concluded: 'The European Parliament is not an organ that represents a sovereign European people.'

It went on: "If a decision in the European Parliament is passed with a narrow majority, there is no guarantee that this majority of votes cast represents the majority of citizens in the EU. For this reason the formation, from within the European Parliament, of an independent government – equipped with the powers that belong to a nation state – raises fundamental objections. It is possible that a numerical minority of citizens can rule through a majority of European members of parliament, against the political will of an opposition of citizens in the Union who do not feel themselves to be represented as a majority."

For this reason, the Court further concluded that the German national parliamentary system would have the final say on any pronouncements relating to the Treaty of Lisbon. And it was only on this basis that the Court was prepared to sanction the Treaty. The European Parliament welcomed the German approval, but the telling comments about its representativeness (or lack of it) were quietly ignored. Because whatever the Germans say, the Parliament still sees itself as the representative of the 'citizens of Europe' and as the indispensible decision-maker of European legislation.

But it is precisely this tendency that makes the 'citizens of Europe' increasingly suspicious about the 'ever-closer Union' – and it is the tragedy of Europe that the European institutional elite fails to recognise this fact.

4

THE 'EVER SOFTER UNION'

If the European dream really exists, then it is to be found in the European Parliament.

The Europe which the majority of MEPs wish to realise is a Europe of limited working hours, good social provisions and state-run programmes against social exclusion. The citizens will be happy in this Europe, and the European Parliament will play an important role in their life, as the source of their prosperity and well-being. It will be a Europe of social stability, with a fully responsible environmental policy, multi-cultural reconciliation and political commitment towards a common project. The 'European model' will set standards for the rest of the world to follow.

The European dream sees Europe as a guide. The old continent, made wiser by its sad experience of war and its besmirched colonial past, will henceforth show other countries the way. Europe is the continent of peace, of tranquil social relationships, of an exemplary record in environmental matters and a close and meaningful relationship with poorer nations. This means that Europe is a pioneer in climate policy and Third World aid. To prove that these are just not fine words, between 2008 and 2013 Europe will make 22.6 billion euros available to support countries in Africa, the Caribbean and the Pacific Basin. Europe is a generous giver, but it needs to be, if it wishes to prove its sincerity – and persuade others to follow. Europe's ambition is global, and its ambitions will be reached through the European method. But is Europe still a global power?

If the idea of the 'ever closer Union' is the EU's guiding principle within its own boundaries, the idea of 'soft power' is its counterpart outside its home continent. Europe consults, advises, feeds and subsidises across the globe. Having learnt the hard lessons of imperial history, Europe implements these processes without threat, force or overt display of political strength. Europe practises politics without power, so that its good example might serve as an inspiration to others. In the eyes of the European institutional elite, soft power allows other countries and their leaders to retain their dignity and worth, and is morally convincing because it is non-aggressive. Soft power – talking, soothing and giving money – is the core of the European diplomatic method. Europe now has a European External Action Service, staffed with officials from the Commission and the Council, supplemented with civil servants from the member nations on detached duty. This effectively means that the EU now has its own foreign and diplomatic service under the leadership of the High Representative of the Union for Foreign Affairs and Security.

For the moment, the effective formation of this external service is being hampered by internal problems of the usual EU kind: manoeuvrings for position, power and prestige. The European Parliament is also sticking its nose into the organisation of the new service, even though it can scarcely organise its own activities. But the 'big guns' of the parliament feel drawn by the 'sacred' quality of its mission. Again, it acts as a *régime d'assemblée*. The external service must grow to become the largest of the Union's common directorates, with European embassies around the world, to serve as its antennae.

The European dream of Strasbourg's parliamentarians places Europe in two different central roles. Firstly, the European model will be normative for other continents, which must also form regional blocs. Secondly, Europe's standing in the world will be based on ethical politics. European values are universal values – it is simply that the Chinese and the Africans haven't realised it yet. Europe must play a pioneering role, which will help to make this clear to them.

Does this European dream correspond to reality? While the dream is legitimate and even praiseworthy, it is impossible to practise international politics without the use of power. The world is a stage where superpowers – and lesser ones – compete with each other for markets, raw materials and technological knowledge. Nations or groups of nations that are motivated by an exaggerated idealism will be laughed at – and pushed to one side. Diplomatic naivety actually encourages distrust and a cynical response.

If it follows this route, Europe will be marginalised, because soft power is essentially without content, unless it is backed by a concrete source of strength. In other words, soft power only works if hard power – economic or military – is waiting in the wings: first the carrot, but then the stick, if necessary. Soft power on its own is an almost pathetic gesture, more likely to be greeted with laughter than respect. It doesn't lead to peace, but to appeasement.

The European elite is reluctantly starting to realise that this moralistic, almost missionary, Euro-centrist approach has had its day. With the gravitational shift of economic and political power from the Atlantic Ocean to the Pacific Ocean, Europe is finding itself increasingly on the fringe of world affairs. This has been a gradual process, but it is now clearly visible. Other leading nations, such as America, China, India and Brazil, work hard and unashamedly to secure their economic interests. They have more to occupy their minds than Europe's morality tales. They consider Europe to be preachy, pedantic and the epitome of moral arrogance. In short, Europe lacks the legitimacy to play the moral guide.

This fact came painfully to the surface during the Copenhagen Conference in December 2009. The EU looked forward optimistically to this gathering about global warming. It expected to play a leading part in the formation of an 'ambitious' climate policy: a 20% reduction in carbon emissions by 2020 in comparison with 1990, or, "if the circumstances are favourable", even a 30% reduction. Europe also planned to highlight its 20% target for renewable energy by 2020, a laudable objective, which it again hoped would serve to inspire others. In keeping with its desire to be at the forefront of the proceedings, Europe reserved eleven places for MEPs who would act as 'observers' at the negotiations. In reality, 110 members eventually went to Copenhagen, not only to observe, but also to take part in the discussions and even to co-negotiate. The corridors were very quiet in Brussels that week – everyone had caught the plane to Denmark! Those who stayed behind were disappointed to miss what everyone was confident would be 'an historic moment'.

And indeed, Copenhagen was historic – but not quite in the way the European Parliament had in mind.

The conference was a huge affair, with almost 50,000 participants. Together, they could have filled a football stadium, and this might have been a better way to spend their time. The large numbers made organisation impractical, if not impossible.

The EU was not alone in sending a large delegation. Most of the 27 Member States also sent sizeable contingents. As might be expected, Belgium – with its six governments, 60 ministers and almost 500 members of various parliaments – had one of the largest delegations. Amongst its members was the Minister of the Environment for the Brussels Region, Evelyn Huytebroeck. She received an unpleasant surprise when it became known during the conference that the crucial Brussels water purification station had not been working for a number of weeks. As a result, sewage from Brussels, the capital city of the European Union, was being pumped unrefined into the waters of the River Zenne and the River Schelde. Both rivers had become seriously polluted and their fish populations were all but decimated. Huytebroeck said that there was nothing she could do about it, and so she decided to stay in Copenhagen. Having done so, she proceeded to lecture the Chinese about their appalling environmental record and said that they should be threatened with EU sanctions if they did not immediately follow the European model. The Chinese delegation – which in relative terms was much smaller than the Belgian one – were not amused at having to listen to this from a dignitary who was allowing the waterways of her capital to fill up with untreated effluent from all the city's toilets. It seemed to confirm all they had ever suspected about European arrogance.

In the eyes of many, Europe received her just desserts for this type of behaviour when it became known that America, China, India, Brazil and South Africa had struck a separate deal, away from the main conference. The text of this deal encouraged the participating countries to reduce their carbon emissions by 'an agreed percentage' in comparison with the figures for 2005. The countries were free to fill in their own 'agreed percentage', and the 2005 basis was much higher than the 1990 figures which the EU used for its own planned 20% reduction.

Even America only joined in on the deal at the last moment, when President Obama accidentally stumbled into a secret meeting between the Chinese, the Indians and the Brazilians. But Europe, for all its huge delegations, was left completely out in the cold. It was a *fait accompli*. There was nothing else to do but pack their bags and fly home. All they had contributed to, ironically, was their own carbon footprint. So much for the idea of a guiding role!

The failure and humiliation of Copenhagen threw the European Parliament into a mood of depression. In the corridors, there was nothing but unhappy faces and puzzled looks. 'Something had gone wrong' was the general conclusion, but nobody knew what. Until, that is, during the Plenary Session in Strasbourg at the beginning of 2010. Suddenly, the nature of the problem became clear: Europe had not been ambitious enough! If Europe wanted to show the world the way, she would have to lead by example – and so instead of aiming for a 20% reduction in emissions by 2020, it was agreed to raise the figure to 30% anyway as a 'signal to the world'. Surely that would convince the Chinese and the Indians that Europe occupied the moral high-ground. Wouldn't it?

While the MEPs were moaning about the failure of Copenhagen, and above all about their own marginalisation, they either missed or ignored another important development that had been taking place. Shortly before the conference began, the scientific evidence on which the theory of global warming is based began to melt away, quicker than a polar ice cap. Intercepted e-mails between researchers at the University of East Anglia in Great Britain and the University of Pennsylvania in the United States suggested that certain key statistics that did not fit in with this theory had been quietly suppressed. There was talk of 'manipulated data' and of pressure being applied to make sure that voices which were critical of the theory of global warming were kept firmly in their place.

The British climate researcher Phil Jones admitted to a British parliamentary committee in 2010 that the e-mails had been 'pretty naughty', and that he had withheld certain information, so as 'not to play into the hands of those who deny global warming'.

These same scientists were responsible for the provision of academic data for the IPCC report, which the United Nations had published in 2007. That year, the IPCC – together with Al

Gore, the ex-vice-president of the United States, who had been elevated to the status of an environmental icon – were awarded the Nobel Prize for Peace. After the Jones e-mails were leaked, people began to look more closely at the IPCC report. Some of their contentions were shown not to be true, such as the rate at which the glaciers in the Himalayas are supposed to be melting, or the shrinkage of the Amazon rain forest, or the levels of crop yield in Africa. They had also claimed that 55% of the Netherlands is under sea level, whereas every Dutch schoolchild knows that the actual figure is just 25%.

It is striking that these errors, which date from 2007, were only revealed in 2010: apparently the report had such good credentials of believability that nobody actually bothered to check the facts. After Copenhagen, however, the revelation of dozens of other factual inconsistencies led to the complete discrediting of the IPCC claims. The scientists had used evidence and sources which had not been scientifically checked, but which fitted in neatly with the theories they wanted to support. In short, they behaved like activists.

You might expect that these disclosures would lead to a serious debate in the European Parliament about its climate policy. But no, the few members who tried to raise the issue were shouted down, almost as if they had been advocating Holocaust denial instead of global warming denial. The majority of MEPs continue to cling fast to the existing theory, notwithstanding the facts and the faults. No one wants to be bothered by new inconvenient truths. Why? Because Europe's 'exemplary' climate policy is based on the findings of the IPCC report.

Whoever casts doubt on the theory, origins or speed of global warming is accused of muddying the waters, so that the whole EU policy edifice might come tumbling down. And this could never be accepted – because the Union's climate programme is a shining example to the rest of the planet.

In other words, the European Union is continuing to build a climate policy on the basis of scientific evidence that is no longer credible. It will carry on with this policy, alone if necessary, since this is the only possible way to convince the unbelieving world to follow its brave lead. But while the faith is still strong in Strasbourg and Brussels, many of Europe's citizens are beginning to have their doubts. The EU and the environmental activists may continue to support the IPCC claims, but the north-east of the United States and Europe have just experienced one of the coldest winters in many years. A number of global warming demonstrations in Copenhagen actually had to be cancelled because of the freezing conditions! Global warming is becoming more and more a question that only concerns the European institutional elite, who have identified themselves too closely with the issue to turn back now, no matter what the facts might say.

In other parts of the world, climate change now occupies a much lower place on the political agenda, while the people of Europe begin to sense that they have been the victim of unnecessary scare tactics by their own representatives. But the Union's politicians and officials are oblivious to all this, and still see the climate issue as a source of moral self-satisfaction and self-justification. That it no longer reflects reality is not relevant. It reflects the reality of the political-bureaucratic complex – and that is the only reality that counts.

The conference in Copenhagen also exploded the myth that Europe speaks with one voice on climate matters. There were so many government leaders in Denmark that you might have been forgiven for thinking that a state funeral or a royal wedding was about to take place.

The Treaty of Lisbon promised to provide a solution for this 'too many cooks' scenario. It was decided to appoint a President of Europe and a High Representative for Foreign Affairs and Security.

The European Council chose the Belgian Premier Herman Van Rompuy to be the Permanent President of the Council, although people more popularly refer to the post – as I did in the previous paragraph – as the President of Europe. The British Lady Ashton was chosen as the face of Europe's foreign policy. It is noticeable that Europe's political leaders selected relatively anonymous figures to fill both of these key positions, presumably to prevent them from stealing all the political limelight. France, in particular, pushed the Van Rompuy bid, because of his modesty and his apparent desire to serve and be servile towards others. These are qualities that President Sarkozy admires in other politicians, even though he does not necessarily possess them himself. Lady Ashton was a kind of last-minute choice, after no other serious candidates could be found. She happened to be fifth choice which means that four high-ranking Brits declined the job. Ashton was a bit of consolation for the British and the Socialists after the rejection of the Blair candidacy for the president's job. Unsurprisingly, Blair would have tried to outshine other political leaders; a fatal mistake in Brussels which is dominated by grey, rather unknown figures. So, the dynamic duo – Van Rompuy and Ashton – are now supposed to put Europe on the world map.

First indications, however, suggest that the number of European cooks has not diminished. During the Plenary Session of the European Parliament in January 2010, the 'rotating' President of the European Union – the Spanish Premier José Zapatero – made a speech praising this concept of a rotating presidency, while a permanent president – in the person of Van Rompuy – had only been appointed two months before! Fortunately he was not in the chamber; otherwise the confusion would have been complete. In other words, Europe now has two presidents: a rotating one, who sets and organises the Union's agenda for a six month period, and a permanent one, who provides continuity in the Union's policy over a longer period of five years. This is characteristic of the bureaucratic approach of the EU to almost every situation. If there is a problem – too many cooks – it is solved by... creating another cook! This time, a super-cook: a permanent President of the Council of Europe. Instead of removing the old bureaucratic layer (the rotating presidency), a new one (the permanent presidency) is simply superimposed on top of it.

But if it will be hard enough to give Van Rompuy's job a clear profile, it will be even harder for the High Representative. There is no likelihood that the three major EU countries – Germany, France and Great Britain – will deliver their foreign policy into the gentle hands of Lady Ashton. A common European foreign policy is certainly desirable, but in reality that will only be possible when the 'Big Three' all agree on the same line. If they don't agree, they will simply follow their own course, which may run in a completely different direction from Ashton's. In other words, 'common' is a relative term, when applied to the Union's foreign policy.

Nowhere was this clearer than in the run-up to the Iraq War in 2003. Great Britain was in favour of the invasion of Iraq, whereas France and Germany were against it. There was absolutely no question of a common position, and the then High Representative, Javier Solana, had nothing to say on the matter. However, in matters where there is greater unity of opinion – for example, reaction to the Iranian nuclear programme – there is indeed a basis for a common approach. However, it remains to be seen whether Iran – which is currently trying to create hard power in the form of a nuclear bomb – will be impressed by Europe's jaw-jaw, soft power approach. More probably, Iran is using the European talking method simply to buy time.

The marginalisation of Europe was also evident in the decision of President Obama not to attend the scheduled EU-US summit. This was another instance where the rotating and permanent presidents seemed to get under each other's feet. And this is before we have even mentioned the President of the European Parliament and the President of the European Commission!

In other words, Europe has four presidents, and they all like to have their say! Instead of a single mouthpiece, there are four competing mouthpieces, each responsible for different aspects of the European apparatus and each keen to get their face on television as often as possible.

The President of the European Council (Van Rompuy) and the President of the European Commission (Barroso) have now agreed to travel abroad together, as a single EU delegation. Van Rompuy will discuss matters that fall within the remit of the Council (Afghanistan, for example) and Barosso will discuss matters for which the Commission is exclusively responsible (such as foreign trade). Joint competences – such as energy – will be 'divided equally' between them – by a process as yet undefined. No wonder Obama cancelled his visit: he would have first needed to follow a crash course in European law, and even then he would have had no idea who he would be likely to meet on the other side of the negotiating table.

But there is more to Obama's current indifference than the confused nature of the European decision-making process. He is more irritated by Europe's lack of will to 'go the extra mile', once the limits of soft power have been reached. Obama wants to see more European troops in Afghanistan, but the European leaders are reluctant. Worse still, they are actively pulling the plug. The Dutch decided to withdraw their forces at the beginning of 2010. The Belgians are doing little more than guarding the airport in Kabul. A smart move: if things go wrong, at least they will be the first ones to get out. Afghanistan is not an 'American' war, but is an operation sanctioned by the United

Nations Security Council, with the reconstruction of the country as its purpose. However, America is shouldering an increasingly heavy load (both in terms of resources and blood), while most of its European 'partners' are attempting to cut and run. Obama is popular in Europe, but this is not reflected in concrete support for his policies.

And the European strategy of trying to talk their opponents into submission is starting to get on his nerves. In Europe, what you say is more important than what you do. In America, actions still speak louder than words. Not that Obama himself always gets things right. He sent a bust of Winston Churchill (a present from Prime Minister Blair to President Bush) back to London – an insensitive gesture, particularly in view of the fact that Churchill's mother was American. He also addressed a letter intended for President Sarkozy to his predecessor – and political rival – Jacques Chirac. These are not huge mistakes, but they are symptomatic of a lack of understanding and empathy. If an American president wants to succeed in Europe, he must show respect to the British, charm the French and cuddle the Germans. Obama still has plenty of political credit in Europe, perhaps even more than in America. But he is doing very little with it. His thinking is purely utilitarian: if the Europeans can do nothing for me, to hell with them.

Soft power, almost by definition, leads to declaratory politics. Europe talks and talks and talks – and then talks some more. Even with the very worst dictators. Amongst the leaders present at the Afro-European Summit held in Lisbon in 2007 was President Robert Mugabe of Zimbabwe. Despite the fact that he has officially been banned from setting foot in the EU since he was found to have rigged the elections of 2002, his European hosts were too scared to deny him entry into Lisbon, in case this led to a wider African boycott. This might not have been such a bad thing, since many of these leaders talk about contributing to the development of their countries whilst at the same time systematically stripping them of their wealth and resources. Only Great Britain and The Netherlands had the courage to criticise Mugabe during the meeting. His so-called EU ban became an outstanding example of Brussels' pointless declaratory approach.

The Libyan leader, Moammar Gadaffi, is another of Europe's conversation partners. Some years ago he was received as a guest by the President of the Commission, Romano Prodi, and since then continues to do business with European governments as though the 1988 Lockerbie outrage – when Libyan agents blew up an American Pam-Am jet over a Scottish town – had never happened. Even the British government is talking to him again, and recently let one of the bombers out of prison, although London left the matter in the hands of the Scottish Minister of Justice, who apparently also defines British foreign policy.

Since the United States invaded Iraq and allowed its Baghdad sympathisers to put Saddam Hussein on the end of a hangman's rope, Gadaffi has been more circumspect in his direct criticism of America. For this reason, he now chooses to vent his spleen on European countries instead. Italy is a favourite target. Libya let thousands of African asylum-seekers sail un-hindered from its coast towards Italy, the nearest European land. This actually turned Gadaffi into the world's largest hu-man trafficker, but far from being ashamed by this, he tried to turn the situation to his advantage. He told the Italians that he would stop the flood of refugees, if they signed a 'treaty of part-nership', in which the Italians would recognise the 'crimes' committed during their colonial occupation of Libya and pay five billion euros in compensation. This was a joke that even the ever-laughing Silvio Berlusconi failed to appreciate, but the Italian prime minister had little option. The Italians signed and paid up.

After Italy, it was Switzerland's turn. The Swiss do not be-long to the EU, but they are members of the Schengen Zone (which allows them free movement with EU countries belong-ing to that zone). They had the temerity to lock up Gadaffi's son, after he had beaten up his household staff in Geneva. Gadaffi Senior was furious, and threatened Switzerland with an immediate oil embargo. He also locked up Swiss citizens in Libya, without due cause or process. In the meantime, he has declared 'holy war' against the Swiss, who presumably did not win his favour with their recent ban on minarets.

Where was Europe's Common Foreign and Security Policy while all this was going on? 'Nowhere', is the answer. Africa is a 'difficult' continent for the EU, because of the many unresolved associations with Europe's colonial past. Put simply, the Euro-peans feel guilty – and they try to relieve their guilt by tolerating the ravings of African dictators and paying huge amounts of cash in development aid. In this respect, the EU is the largest donor organisation in the world.

In 2009, the European Court of Auditors concluded (in its 4/2009 report) that one billion euros of the money spent or donated by non-governmental organisations was offering cause for concern. This is equivalent to 10% of the total aid budget! Many of the projects were judged to be 'non-sustainable', and collapsed once the funding stopped. The European Parliament met to discuss this situation at the end of 2009. But instead of carpeting the NGOs and insisting on a more responsible use of tax-payers' money, they meekly accepted the NGOs' own claims that more money was needed: to hold more conferences and to appoint more officials, so that <u>then</u> a more efficient policy could be developed.

Even in Africa, it seems, 'more Europe' is the answer to every problem. The Court of Auditors' report caused almost no comment in the Parliament. Apparently, the quality of aid is not so important, as long as the EU retains its status as the 'largest donor', as the last resort of soft power.

But soft power also has other tools at its disposal: resolutions, for example. In recent years, the European Parliament has passed dozens of resolutions, bemoaning the sorry state of affairs in different parts of the world.

These resolutions usually relate to human rights violations, in countries such as Iran, China, Burma, Tibet, Congo, Yemen, the Gaza Strip or Uzbekistan. Nobody disputes that human rights represent fundamental and universal values and that their violation should be combated, wherever possible. But it is not unreasonable to question whether the passing of a resolution on an almost monthly basis does much to help the situation, if there is no concrete action to back the resolutions up.

Every Plenary Session places one or more of the offending nations in the public pillory. But if the resolution had no effect last time, why should it have any effect this time? It is also noticeable that the further away the country is located from Europe, the easier it is for the Parliament to agree a text. And the less the Parliament knows about a country, the more strident its denunciation. Declaratory politics has its limits, certainly if the EU finds itself marginalised in future.

The European Parliament would be better advised to focus its attention on a condition without which it is impossible to conduct any kind of common foreign policy: energy independence. The EU is currently dependent for its supplies of energy on many of the countries it is so busy criticising, such as Russia and the Arab states. In 2007, the 27 EU member states imported 82% of their oil needs and 60% of their gas. As far as oil is concerned, a third of the supply comes from the Middle East (including 10% from Libya) and a third from Russia. Russia also supplies 40% of the gas. This energy dependence turns the concept of an independent European foreign policy into an illusion. As a result, the EU has to beg for energy, which makes its foreign policy even softer. In short, the EU is becoming the 'ever softer Union'.

Energy independence is of great strategic importance, and the only realistic way to achieve this independence is through the further development of nuclear power. Reducing energy consumption and tapping alternative energy sources all help, but only nuclear power is capable of producing the levels of energy that can break Europe's reliance on external, foreign supply.

This means that a revised nuclear development programme must become a key part of the European energy mix. But nobody in the EU dares to take the step, even though energy is now a shared competence under the Treaty of Lisbon. The Barroso-1 Commission produced a green book for energy policy which didn't even mention nuclear power. And the same trend is evident in the European Parliament. For example, the Parliament has 28 intergroups. These are themed work groups, in which MEPs from different political party groupings come together to discuss topics of common interest. There are currently intergroups for biodiversity, hunting, wine (very popular!), animal welfare, water, mountainous regions, the Western Sahara, Tibet and transsexual rights. All that is necessary to set up an intergroup is the support of at least three party groupings. But when it was proposed to set up an intergroup for nuclear energy, it was impossible to find three groupings willing to join. Nuclear power was regarded as too controversial a topic, which would only spoil the 'harmonious relations within the parliament'.

It is the same old story. The European Parliament concerns itself with almost everything you can think of, other than the great strategic issues of our time. It is almost like playing at politics.

The most extreme form of Euro-centrism in the European Parliament is reserved for matters relating to the United States. If Europe can show that it stands on the other side of the fence from America – even the America of Barack Obama – the Parliament usually celebrates this as some kind of victory.

The motion to allow the US access to European bank transactions –the so-called Swift agreement – was defeated by 378 votes to 196 votes, with 31 abstentions. This meant that the US was denied the opportunity to examine European bank records, in the hope of tracking down terrorist groups. The Swift agreement was portrayed in Parliament as though it gave the Americans the right to examine the banking details of every person, company and organisation in Europe. But this was not the case. In reality, they only asked for access to the records of persons who were suspected of planning terrorist activities. In security circles, this procedure results from 'profiling' possible suspects and following their money trail. In fact, it was through following a trail of bank transactions that it was finally possible to arrest the architect of the Bali bombings in 2002, when more than 200 people were killed. Using the same techniques, several planned attacks on airports have also been foiled. It was for this reason that the European Commission and most of the Member States supported the Swift agreement with the United States.

But their opinions made no difference: the Parliament rejected Swift anyway, basing their decision on the principle of privacy. Yet the Swift agreement actually offered greater safeguards for privacy than the possible alternative; namely, 27 separate agreements between the US and the individual EU member states. In that case, the US simply dictates the terms.

The real reason for the vote was not love of privacy, but ideological dislike of Uncle Sam. The left-wing groupings in the Parliament shouted and cheered in jubilation when the result was announced. They had won! But what had they won? They had won against the Americans – and that was all that mattered. You are unlikely to see scenes of this kind in the American Senate, if, for example, they turn down a pro-European proposal. But it is a very different matter on the other side of the Pond. The more Europe can distance itself from America, the more unified it becomes.

In similar fashion, the record fine imposed by the European Commission on Microsoft was seen by many as 'Europe sending a powerful signal'. The EU had actually done something, had justified its existence for once. Leaving aside the issue of whether or not the imposition of the fine was legally correct, you never hear the same kinds of admonitory arguments being used when fines are imposed on Japanese companies.

But as soon as America is involved, Europe's emotions become heated and reason flies out of the window. In reaction to the financial crisis in Greece, European politicians launched the idea of setting up a European Monetary Fund. An International Monetary Fund (IMF) exists and EU countries already contribute to it precisely for the purpose of helping nations in financial trouble. But some European leaders consider the IMF to be too American. True, the IMF headquarters are in Washington, but the chairman is always a European! Even so, there is a perception that the Americans use the IMF to manipulate the euro – and so there needs to be a separate EMF. And what is the difference between the EMF and the IMF? There is only one difference: America.

The psychological explanation for this phenomenon is not simple, but it comes down to the fact that the European institutional elite defines itself by the extent to which it can distance itself from the USA. This is the result of an inferiority complex, which is particularly deep-rooted in the European Parliament. During debates there are often references to 'the American way of doing things', but always in a negative sense, focusing on stereotyped images of American society: unbridled capitalism, greedy lawyers, stupid politicians, fat citizens, fraudulent bankers, conservative priests, gangs of Hispanics roaming the streets, Republicans, etc.

The Bush presidency gave a huge impulse to this nascent anti-American feeling, since he seemed to amalgamate so many of these 'qualities' in his own person! The Norwegian Parliament awarded four anti-Bush Nobel Prizes for Peace: Jimmy Carter, Al Gore, Paul Krugman and Barack Obama. The decision to award the Prize to Obama had already been taken before he was inaugurated as President on January 20, 2009! He hadn't done anything yet, let alone achieved noble goals. What is noble to Norway? It is not a member of the EU, but likes to present itself as a feminist model state, which thanks to its deep oil fields and rich fish stocks – safe beyond the reach of the European Common Fishing Policy – is in the luxurious position of trying to educate the world. The Nobel Prize for Peace is its chosen method. Norway, our world guide!

Even after the election of the more 'liberal' Obama, the left of the European Parliament (in particular, but not exclusively) is still of the opinion that America is not 'a good thing'. This feeling is strengthened still further whenever the Republicans make electoral progress, like in the autumn of 2009. The European press – which (apparently) also forms part of our political cultural elite – usually helps to intensify the effect. In 2008, I covered the American presidential elections as a journalist and often travelled on the campaign bus with other European reporters. I have seldom experienced such a concentration of vitriolic anti-American sentiment, although there were a few notable exceptions. Their opinions can be summarised as follows: all Republicans are dangerous fools, the Midwest is populated by some very creepy farmers, the South is inherently racist and Fox News is a quasi-Nazi broadcaster. Even Hillary Clinton, when compared to the iconic Obama, was a bitch, whereas the mere mention of the name Sarah Palin had everybody reaching for the sick bags. In short, according to the European press corps, half of the country is certifiably bonkers.

How can European journalists report on a country that they don't understand? Little wonder that European public opinion is so prejudiced against America if the newspapers are full of this kind of nonsense. I have seldom felt so alone as I felt on that campaign bus. It is not an experience that I am anxious to repeat.

Euro-centrism leads to a moral arrogance for which there is no longer any underlying political power base. In its desire to give a moral lead, Europe profiles itself as an alternative to America. And although Europe no longer is an alternative to the US in military and economic terms, it still draws support from many of the world's other political elites.

China still needs an anti-American posture to remind its huge population of the 'horrors' of freedom; in Arab countries, an external bogey-man is necessary to mask the failure of their own ruling elites; the same is true in Africa, but this time to conceal the massive corruption of tin-pot dictators; and in South America, it is simply a means to bolster the self-image and self-respect of the various caudillos. But in all these instances, anti-American sentiment is largely confined to the governing class. You will find little trace of it amongst the ordinary people.

How do I know? Ask yourself this question: if Africans, Chinese, Latin Americans or Arabs get the chance to emigrate, where do they want to emigrate to? America! Why? The American dream is a universal dream of freedom shared by most people: "Life, liberty and the pursuit of happiness." They want no more than this, since this is all they never had. In contrast, the European dream is restricted to the European institutional elite. Resistance to a self-created image of 'Americanisation' is necessary to justify their role as moral guide. 'Just look how much better things are in Europe!'

But is it true? And will Europe still be able to say it in 2020, notwithstanding the EU 2020 strategy? In the meantime, New York has become one of the safest places in the world, while in Brussels, the capital of Europe, some parts of the city are subject to a night curfew. Even MEPs living in the Schumann quarter have been robbed and beaten up on the streets, while the Brussels police are nowhere to be seen. And the situation is much the same in Amsterdam, Paris, Berlin and London. 'Things are better in Europe.' Are they?

5

THE EVER BIGGER BUDGET

In origin, parliaments were bodies which protected the people from power-mad and money-mad kings, who were forever imposing new taxes. Nowadays, parliaments are launching state expenditure to new heights, and the European Parliament is no exception to this rule. The only difference is that the citizens – who still have to pay the taxes – are now unprotected.

In a democratic system, the principles of freedom and equality can both be reflected in a nation's fiscal arrangements. Money is the fuel for every government. The government itself is not profit-making but provides in return, if there is good governance, a range of basic services which are important for the society it serves: a road network, education, health care or a safety net of minimum social security.

The government needs income to provide these services, and obtains this income through a series of direct and indirect taxes. A government that offers cheap or free basic services will usually have a high level of taxation, as is the case in the Scandinavian countries. People with high incomes pay proportionately more, with a basic rate of 50% or more for income tax. The citizens themselves have little choice in the matter. It is the state which decides who pays, and how much. This is the standard pattern throughout Western Europe, and many Europeans find the system to be easy and fair. The government takes care of them from 'the cradle to the grave' – and so the welfare state was born.

A government that insists on a lower level of taxation will have no choice but to offer more expensive basic services. This allows the citizens to keep more money in their own pocket, so that they can decide for themselves which services and what quality they are willing to pay for. In other words, the citizen has to make his own contribution towards these services through direct payment. This is the pattern in parts of the United States, and certainly in southern states, such as Texas, Arizona and Florida. In contrast, other states (New York, Illinois, California and New Jersey) have more European levels of taxation and also have a European-style welfare structure. The relative level of taxation is one of the reasons why industrial production in the USA has shifted from the North to the South.

The old American economy with high taxes and strong unions is concentrated in the north-eastern states, the west coast states and the region around the Great Lakes. The new American economy, with low taxes and labour flexibility, is concentrated in the South. Detroit is the heart of the US car manufacturers like Ford, Chrysler and GM. Trade unions like the United Automobile Workers (UAW) are almighty through a system of 'closed shops'. They press for ever-rising wages and benefits. Therefore, European and Japanese car companies have located their factories in southern states like Alabama, Georgia and Tennessee. Boeing, the famous US plane manufacturer domiciled in Washington State on the west coast, decided to produce its supersized Dreamliner in South Carolina, in hard core Dixieland.

As a result, the North is becoming poorer: the state of Michigan has been crippled by economic recession for years. In contrast, the South is getting richer: Dixie is booming! In the previous century, these roles were completely reversed. At the start of this new century, patterns of migration have also been reversed. People are now moving from North to South. States such as New York, California, Illinois, New Jersey and Ohio are seeing their populations reducing at a rapid rate, while densities in Florida, Arizona, Nevada, Georgia, North Carolina and Texas are growing, as a result of internal migration. As always, people make their way to the places where their work is best rewarded – and that is in the states where levels of taxation are the lowest. In 2008, at the start of the recession these migration flows have flattened slightly because the South was equally struck by soaring unemployment.

In European countries and the American states where government intervention creates high levels of taxation and little choice, it is possible to spot a common trend: the government bureaucracy grows, the need for money becomes greater, but the quality of services does not necessarily increase. These governments are following the road towards financial disaster. Most of the West European welfare states have very high levels of taxation – around 50% of GDP goes directly to the state – but nevertheless they experience high levels of state debt and constant budget shortfalls. This pattern was already evident during the prosperous years between 2003 and 2008. In the course of the previous decade, budget deficits in both France and Germany rose above 3% of GDP, the maximum figure set by the Growth and Stability Pact to safeguard the euro. In other words, government expenditure continued to increase faster than the higher revenues it was receiving as a result of economic growth.

The welfare states of Western Europe lack the political will and the necessary degree of social consensus to reduce government expenditure. The citizens pay a great deal, but continue to demand more in return. The government promises to do better, but the range and quality of the services continue to fall. Yet while levels of state debt continue to rise, the state bureaucracy nevertheless continues to grow. The private sector which is supposed to produce the golden eggs is being squeezed out and if it falters, the public sector will become unsustainable and finally collapse. Greece serves as a perfect example.

In their final convulsions, public sector unions will put the government under increasing pressure. They have the ability to disrupt daily life. Moreover, because of their sheer number, they are an important electoral factor. In Great Britain, one million people work in the National Health Service. This means one million votes – or three to four million votes, if you count their family and friends. Similar situations also exist in France, Germany, Italy and Spain. It is also becoming a familiar feature in the American states with a sizeable bureaucratic apparatus, like New York and California. In both Europe and America, there is a constant search for new ways to raise revenue, because the principle of equality cannot assimilate the concept of a 'limited' government. An oversized public sector, once created, can hardly be reined in.

In more difficult times, such as during the economic crisis of 2008, the situation can deteriorate quickly. In this instance, the state needed to set money aside to save the banks that were considered 'too big to fail', although in the meantime most of this money has been paid back. The main problem was to limit the explosion of other state expenditure. In addition to helping the banks, the government also decided to pump money into the economy, in order to maintain levels of economic activity. Since it had been unable to build up a reserve during the prosperous years – a welfare state doesn't know how to save – this money had to be borrowed.

As a result, state debt rose dramatically, while the citizens still demanded an undiminished level of services, creating yet more expenditure and an ever more desperate search for revenue. Several European countries (Greece, Italy and Belgium) have a state debt in excess of 100% of GDP, and most of the others are heading quickly in the same direction. The American federal government has also seen its debt levels climb spectacularly in recent times resulting from budget deficits of Greek proportions, while states such as California and New York are almost bankrupt. The public sectors of both the US and Europe are facing financial meltdown.

At precisely this moment, the Brussels' bureaucrats are brewing a brilliant idea: why not create a new European tax!

What is the dominating view in the ivory towers of the Schuman district in Brussels? The European Union does a lot for its citizens and is extremely 'ambitious'. It would like to do much more, and the bureaucracy could certainly use some extra growth resources. But to do all these things requires money – and the only way to raise lots of money is through taxation and/or by creating further debt through the issue of European bonds. In view of the fact that most of the EU member states are already operating at maximum tax thresholds and are up to their eyes in debt, the bond option is not realistic. And so the European Union now needs to become a new fiscal level for the taxation of Europe's citizens.

In other words, the EU is going to copy the mistakes the European welfare states have already made.

A European tax is the dream of every federalist. Some cherish this dream on the basis of the rather naïve belief that a European tax will bring the EU closer to the people. According to this theory, often heard in Brussels and popular with many Belgian politicians, Europeans will only have a greater common identity, a greater sense of European-ness, if they are paying taxes to the EU. In other words, they are seeking to create a European fiscal identity.

I once had a passionate discussion with former EU Commissioner, Louis Michel, who strongly supported the idea of a European tax 'to bring Europe closer to its citizens'. I warned him that many European citizens would come to Brussels to demonstrate against such a plan, not to welcome it. 'And if you are around, they may even try to decapitate you; that is how close the citizen will come to EU figureheads'. Michel, a seasoned Belgian politician, accused me of being conservative. I replied: 'No Commissioner, I am just trying to save your life'.

Others are cleverer (and certainly shrewder) in their approach. They share the same goals as their more innocent federalist colleagues like Michel, but follow a different reasoning. Achieving the 'ever closer Union' via a European constitution may have failed, but it may still be possible to achieve a fiscal variant via the backdoor, through a system of EU taxation.

Obviously, the European tax must not appear on the pay slip of the European worker, since this would inevitably create a storm of protest and demonstrations in Brussels. For this reason, the tax will need to be disguised – perhaps as a levy on carbon emissions or a charge on each text message, or a tax on financial bank transactions, or an increase in the EU VAT rate. The task of the European Union will be to make very clear to the people what they will be getting in return for this tax-in-disguise.

Within the framework of the current European budget – which for 2010 amounts to 141 billion euros – there is already the seed of a European tax: the so-called own resources. The European Union is financed to the tune of 24% by income that it generates or levies itself, such as Customs duties, sugar tax (for 12%), its proportional share of VAT (for 11%), the taxation of its own European officials, plus fines resulting from infringement of EU competition rules (1%).

The remaining 76% comes from the contributions of the Member States. But the Member States are also pushed for cash, even the net-payers, such as Germany, the Netherlands, Sweden, Belgium, the United Kingdom and Austria. In 2008, Germany contributed 21.5 billion euros to the EU budget – a colossal sum in economically difficult times. The European elite fear that the Member States will eventually seek to reduce their contributions. This is another reason for the growing popularity of the idea to increase 'own resources' through a European tax. This would send a huge stream of money flowing towards Brussels – and in the mental processes of the EU political-bureaucracy complex, more money for the European Union means 'more Europe' for its citizens. This way, the EU can 'do more' in Europe and equally play an important role in the world.

A decision relating to the funding of Europe cannot be postponed indefinitely. The current multi-annual budget, based on 1% of GNI (Gross National Income) of the Union, runs until 2013. The European Commission is dusting off its calculators and is starting to think about the next budgetary plan, which will run until the magical year 2020. With an annually increasing budget based on 1% of EU-GNI – which amounts to 141 billion euros in 2010 – this means that in a seven-year period ending in 2020 the combined budget will have risen to almost one trillion euros. Yet according to Brussels, this is still not enough – at least, not for the 'ambitious' agenda they have in mind.

The number of EU figureheads pleading on behalf of a new European tax is gradually building up. Jose Manuel Barroso, the President of the Commission, is thinking in terms of a levy on electronic text messages. Herman Van Rompuy, the President of the European Council, favours a levy on carbon emissions. The ruling 'pro-European majority' of the European Parliament is inclined to support an EU tax on financial transactions. Guy Verhofstadt, the leader of the Liberals in the European Parliament, is one of the few Liberal leaders I know who is mesmerized (or rather bewitched) by the idea of EU-taxation.

He regards it as an appropriate tool to increase the current EU budget twentyfold, while his compatriot and fellow ex-premier, Jean-Luc Dehaene, has said that Europeans must 'prepare themselves for the idea of a new tax'. Dehaene is a prominent member of the Budgetary Committee of the European Parliament. EU leaders are preparing the ground for EU taxation by influencing the psychological mindset of EU citizens.

As for the Parliament itself, in the past it has always argued in favour of a bigger budget: instead of being satisfied with 1% of EU-GNI, it has long been pressing for a maximum ceiling of 1.24%. If the MEPs had had their way, the budget for 2010 would stand at 170 billion euros. The idea that the European Parliament protects the European taxpayer is a fallacy. Precisely the opposite is true.

What are the tricks the Parliament uses to try and persuade the citizens of Europe that the new tax would work to their benefit? The first argument is that the European tax would be more than compensated for by the abolition of a national tax. This is pure deceit. All the Member States are struggling for funding and there is not a snowball's chance in hell that they will scrap any possible source of revenue. A new European tax would therefore be levied in addition to national taxation, which also looks set to rise still further.

Besides, people are not stupid: they know that this argument is not true. But when they try to speak out, nobody in Brussels or Strasbourg is prepared to listen. The Parliament continues to be the champion of greater European expenditure, because every extra euro is a step towards the 'ever closer Union'.

When dealing with the EU Member States, the European elite uses a different tactic. The payment of national contributions to Brussels to fund the EU budget is always a political tug-of-war. Each country analyses closely what it pays to Europe and what it gets back, via the varions different funds. It is a profit and loss calculation, which at the very least ensures that certain limitations are set on the budget. The most important net payers – with Germany, the United Kingdom and the Netherlands at the forefront – keep a watchful eye to see that things don't get too far out of hand. They will hit the brake whenever they feel that they are contributing too much and receiving too little in return.

Whenever this happens, the net receiver countries (and that is most of the 27 EU member states!) accuse the net payers of a 'lack of solidarity'. For the 2013-2020 period, the payer group is once again being lined up before the firing squad of European public opinion. The demands on them are greater than ever, while their own national finances are becoming ever more strained. Germany, the generous paymaster of Europe, cannot always be expected to pay. And the same accounts for other net payers. They, too, have been hit by the economic crisis, as have their populations, which are becoming increasingly suspicious of the EU subsidy carousel. In the end, the taxpayers will revolt and vote out their government that has been holding them hostage to bail out profligate EU countries.

With this difficult situation likely to erupt in the near future, the European institutional elite has cleverly come up with a new deal for the net payers.

They offer them the option of reducing the proportion of their national budget that is sent to Brussels, provided that instead they are willing to accept the introduction of a European tax of some sort (suitably disguised, of course, as a VAT adjustment, a general levy on electronic traffic or bank transfer, environmental charges, etc.). This allows the national finance ministers to keep more money at home in their own budgets because the contribution to Brussels will indeed be lower, but the cost of this 'budgetary saving' would be transferred to the citizens of each country through EU taxation.

Or to put it in more simple terms: the payer countries are allowed to cut their European losses and the people are taxed behind their backs. For many national finance ministers in these difficult times, it is an offer (to bolster their coffers) that they cannot afford to refuse – providing they can keep the taxpayers of Europe in the dark.

What would be the result of this system? The budgetary brake currently applied by the net paying countries would be circumvented. These governments would have greater funds at their disposal to pay off their growing national debts and reduce their budget deficits. At the same time, the EU could increase the rates of its indirect taxes, initially by small amounts – so the people don't become too alarmed – but then by systematically larger percentages. In the end, the European political-bureaucratic complex would be firmly seated at the EU's fiscal helm.

A European tax would effectively give Brussels an instrument for drawing up its own budget. The European bureaucrats and parliamentarians have long argued for a substantial increase in European expenditure: with a budget based on EU taxation they would at last have the purse strings in their own hands. The net paying countries will have been bought off, while Europe's citizen will be kept sweet with the lie that corresponding national taxes will disappear. But in reality, overall tax rates will increase and the only real winner will be Brussels.

Given this scenario, EU expenditure will rise dramatically. The European bureaucracy will always find new ways of spending the people's money. At the present time, about 45% of the European budget is swallowed up by agricultural and fisheries policy, although this has fallen from a massive 65% in the 1980s. In recent years, expenditure on the Regional Development Fund, the Social Fund, the Cohesion Fund and several other smaller funds has risen considerably. In the 2010 budget, these funds are allocated 49.4 billion euros, whereas agriculture gets 'just' 43.8 billion euros. A further 7.5 billion euros is foreseen for the Seventh Framework Programme for Research and Development and 8.1 billion euros for what can be described as 'Europe's role as a world player': Development aid, assistance to candidate member states, funding for the Common Foreign and Security Policy, etc.

The financial stream for this funding follows the same well-charted course: money is paid by the national treasuries direct to Brussels, where it is reallocated and paid out in accordance with the relevant EU criteria for projects, subsidies and incomes. In other words, it is the Brussels bureaucracy that apportions the money. As a result, this form of financing already gives the bureaucrats great power. A new budget without restrictions would increase that power immeasurably. A European tax can therefore be seen as a first step towards a quasi-European government. And that, of course, is precisely the objective of the 'ever closer Union'. Honestly speaking, I am unable to accuse the European institutional elite of inconsistency. They are consistent, although mistakenly.

The European Parliament is not really of much use or interest to the citizens of Europe. This is bad enough, but the Parliament now wants to encourage the European Commission to make the situation even worse. According to the Treaty of Lisbon, the Parliament now has co-decision powers over the entire EU budget. Initially, that authority was restricted to noncompulsory expenditure, but over the years the parliament's influence on the budget has grown systematically. With the Lisbon Treaty, its powers are now greater than even the Parliament itself realises. Budgetary affairs are not 'sexy' in Europe and very few people actually understand how the EU budget procedure works.

But as soon as the European Parliament begins to realise the true implications of its new budgetary powers, the list of proposed projects will explode, since they will seek to enlarge every Commission proposal. This will mean that there must always be more and more money for more and more projects.

The European funds will be overflowing with cash, and every MEP will want to 'do something' for his own Euro-constituency in his native country. A new road, a much-needed bridge, social subsidies: they are all very effective – but costly – methods of getting the folks back home to remember your name. The hand that gives, also takes, votes included. In short, the European Parliament has an escalatory effect on the European budget.

Whether or not this massive flow of extra cash will actually produce beneficial results for the citizens of Europe is another matter. From the bureaucrat's point of view, the acquisition of power is an end in itself. To what extent do the Regional Development Fund, the Cohesion Fund and the Social Fund actually help people in the Member States? Projects subsidised by these funds are only likely to have lasting impact if the fiscal and economic policy of the Member State in question is based on low taxation and on entrepreneurship. In these circumstances, the project – a bridge, a road or an industrial estate – can actually be a useful tool to support effective government policy. But if national economic policy in the Member State is not geared to productive investment or innovative production within a low tax regime, then such projects will have little value: the roads will remain empty and the industrial estates unoccupied. This is nothing more than pumping money through the system – and the few people who benefit are the local contractors who implement the projects. The real added value is minimal. The ultimate winner is of course the pump operator: the EU bureaucracy.

Much the same arguments can be applied to the European Development Fund (EDF). The European Union is the world's largest aid donor, but sending aid to corrupt countries, where the money disappears straight into the pockets (or rather into the Swiss bank accounts) of the ruling elite, serves little purpose. All too often, development aid simply transfers money from poor people in rich countries to rich people in poor countries. One of the biggest landowners in Brazil is the president of Angola. During the Christmas holidays, African elites go shopping in Paris and London, leaving their compatriots behind in utter misery. Nigeria is oil-rich and corruption-ridden, a very familiar combination. Now, African leaders are dealing with China, which cares even less about ordinary Africans.

Fifty years of European aid has achieved relatively few concrete results, if viewed in relation to the level of financial investment. Countries that were poor fifty years ago – such as Ghana or Tanzania – are still poor now, notwithstanding the massive injections of aid that they have received in the intervening period. In contrast, other once 'poor' nations have realised an economic miracle during the same period without significant aid, the classic example being South Korea.

The main difference between these two examples is that South Korea was prepared to modernise and orient its economy to the needs of international trade, while Ghana and Tanzania remained trapped in the old planned economy mentality of the 1950s and 1960s. Development aid is a policy area (or rather a policy error) which is based on factual analyses that were inaccurate – and not always even factual as it was overshadowed by unjustified idealism, wishful thinking and collective guilt feelings. It is hardly surprising, then, that the results should be so limited, in spite of warnings from experts like the famous development economist, Peter Bauer, and the Zambian author, Dambisa Moyo, who have recently published a book with the telling title *Dead Aid*. Currently, the same is true of climate policy, where the factual basis and the analytical assumptions are increasingly subject to question. Even so, the EU wishes to pursue a climate policy that will cost hundreds of millions of euros. Once bureaucratically established, a policy area driven by good intentions is hard to change, even if it appears to be erroneous.

The European Programme for Research and Development can at least offer the excuse that it is vital for the future of Europe. Nobody would dispute that innovation and technological development are necessary. Projects that involve cooperation between research institutions in different Member States are eligible for subsidies. But this is where a common EU problem arises. The subsidy application is so complex and bureaucratic that the initiative-takers get bogged down in paperwork and often need to engage the services of (expensive) subsidy specialists and lobbyists to get their project over the EU obstacle course.

This is probably true for every subsidy application in the EU, but the problem is more severe for the R&D sector, because of the technical nature of their projects. Researchers are widely known for their patience and perseverance, and they need all these qualities and more when dealing with the Brussels bureaucrats. Even so, the resulting delays often mean that money is allocated too late to be of any use: either the project has already collapsed through lack of funds, or has been successfully completed without Europe's help.

In reality, the European Union does not really need such an extensive budget. Agricultural expenditure could be cut to 40% without too much difficulty and the fast growing Regional Development Fund could be restricted to help for the poorest areas in the poorest member states. So, the poorest EU member states would still get their various EU subsidies in the timeframe 2013-2020 whilst accepting that the richer EU states are better positioned to develop their own poorer regions than the mandarins in Brussels. If they can't do it themselves, what chance does Europe have?

Nevertheless, bureaucracies always prefer subsidies to tax cuts. The former give power, while the latter take it away. Even so, surely there must still be room for a low tax regime for the poorest areas of Europe? Lower taxes attract investors. This was the key to the Irish economic success story in recent years. Put another way, low taxes have made Ireland rich. Moreover, it was a process in which subsidies from Brussels played only a marginal role. This is a concept that the Brussels bureaucrats find hard to understand: according to their logic, it is subsidies – and not reduced levels of taxation – which bring power and success.

But low tax could also prove useful in other ways; for example, for inter-company ventures or cross-border R&D projects.

Paying less tax can have a direct beneficial effect, whereas waiting for subsidies can sometimes take years of jumping through bureaucratic hoops. The objective must be to keep costs low at source and that is what a tax cut does. This golden rule has proved its value time after time, and is now accepted by everyone – apart from the European elite. A similar strategy could also be applied to development aid. Instead of setting up extensive and unsustainable projects in donor countries, give these countries access to European markets, give easy access to venture capital, promote entrepreneurship and offer them a reduced tax regime. In short: trade, not aid.

Tax reduction is indisputably a more effective political instrument than subsidisation, but no bureaucracy in the world will ever be prepared to concede this fact. For them, subsidies mean power. As soon as proposals for tax cuts begin to appear, the EU institutional elite says that what we really need is 'tax harmonisation'. This, for example, is what happened when the last twelve new member states joined the Union. Most of these countries had experienced Communist regimes during the Soviet era, and therefore had no well defined taxation system, since all the means of production had effectively been in the hands of the state. In these circumstances, personal income was almost a kind of gift from the state towards its citizens, and the national budget was a giant subsidy fund. This explains why many Central and East European countries introduced a flat tax after the fall of Communism.

There was a single tariff, usually around 20%, for both personal tax and company tax. This meant that when these countries joined the EU, their level of company tax was significantly below the EU's average, which runs at about 35%. France and Germany immediately demanded that tax rates should be harmonised, in order to avoid a 'race to the bottom'. The newcomers were not willing to play ball, and so the West European giants had little option but to begin cutting their own levels of company tax – with positive effects on competitiveness and economic development. So, tax competition – rather than tax harmonisation – is actually an effective means of preventing a 'race to the top'.

And so where does all this leave the citizens of Europe? As usual, taxpayers are left holding the baby. If the European Commission and the European Parliament can persuade the member states to accept the idea of a European tax, in return for the reduction of national contributions, the European citizen will once again be sacrificed on the altar of European 'ambition'.

The European bureaucracy will increase every aspect of its financial operations: tax rates, budgets and subsidies. This new EU fiscal regime will further promote the equality principle by boosting fiscal revenues, unsurprisingly at the expense of the freedom principle. Money and power will flow towards Brussels. The budget will succeed where the European Constitution failed. This will allow Brussels to make all the mistakes that the world's welfare states have already made in the past. The EU will acquire the powers and the financial means to establish an uncontrollable income redistribution mechanism which will ultimately create and expand unaffordable entitlements schemes. Commonsensical politics is about putting 'incentives' in the right place, but the EU political bureaucratic system will instinctively do precisely the opposite by means of EU taxation.

For the European Union, this will be the beginning of the end of its legitimacy. For the European citizen, the primacy of the equality principle and the repression of human ingenuity will generate the beginning of state-sponsored poverty.

The peoples of Europe must wake up to the fact that a European tax will herald an era of 'soft despotism', in which government will be in the hands of a self-perpetuating institutional elite, increasingly demanding more money and more power.

If citizens want to do something about this, they must do it now – before it is too late.

6

THE EVER MORE POWERLESS PEOPLE

There is no other public organisation in the world that refers so frequently to the citizens as the European Union – and there is no other public organisation where the citizen has so little to say. The European ideal has been bureaucratised and has now entered the phase of micro-management. In its ivory Tower of Babel, the EU sends out one directive after another, influencing the daily lives of people at the farthest corners of the continent. Its 'good intentions' lead to 'unintended consequences', but these are quietly swept under the carpet. The citizen can only look on impotently. Or perhaps not: are there not ways in which they can influence the European process from the bottom up?

The Treaty of Lisbon offers one or two faint rays of hope. The treaty refers to the principle of subsidiarity, a concept that is often preached but seldom practised. In matters that lie outside its full competence, the European Union is only empowered to act 'if and in so far as' the objectives in question cannot be realised by the Member States alone. Moreover, in such circumstances the Union must bear in mind a degree of proportionality in its actions and must not exceed 'what is reasonable'.

But in reality these provisions are hardly ever observed. The system defines its own sphere of operations and its own definition of 'what is reasonable'. For the European institutional elite, everything is important and always demands an 'ambitious' agenda. This process is beyond the reach of the citizens and cannot be influenced by them. The principle of subsidiarity was first written into the Maastricht Treaty of 1992 as a safeguard against the level of power that the political union might acquire. However, the safeguard was actually meaningless, since the necessity for a particular piece of legislation is effectively determined by the legislator.

All aspects of European law fall under the Court of Justice and the Court interprets this law 'in the spirit of the treaties', which means in the spirit of the 'ever closer Union'. If the European Parliament and the Council of Ministers do not agree on the precise wording of essential provisions in EU draft legislation they tend to compromise on a vague, watery text often provided by the European Commission, the master of Vatican-like language. Within years, the vaguely formulated provision creates legal disputes and ends up on the doorstep of the Court of Justice in Luxembourg. Whatever the intricacies of the wording, the Court will resort to the philosophy of the 'ever closer Union' as its guiding spirit and, if need be, legislate from the bench. That is precisely what the Parliament and the Commission want, while washing their hands in innocence. So, Maastricht did not establish an effective subsidiarity test.

For this reason, the Treaty of Lisbon built in a second safeguard to protect the principle of subsidiarity. The Treaty requires the Commission to forward its proposals for legislation to the national parliaments of the Member States. These parliaments have two months in which to submit comments and recommendations. In particular, they must examine whether or not the proposal relates to a matter which perhaps could be better dealt with by the national administrations.

Put more bluntly, the national parliaments can decide whether or not the Commission is trying to stick its nose where it doesn't belong. This is really a kind of subsidiarity test. National parliaments can sound the alarm bell if they think their jurisdiction is being infringed – but will they actually do so? The two month period is very short and the warning system has only a relative value.

Every parliament is a hornet's nest of conflicting interests and rival prejudices, which are often turned inwards, rather than outwards. Within this context, Europe is important, but not very important for their media profile in national politics. It is more of a side issue than a central issue. Moreover, few national politicians have experience of Europe and they are unaware of the Machiavellian workings of the Brussels bureaucracy – until it is too late.

In theory, the ordinary citizen can also press the alarm button via his regional MEP, but he is even less able to interpret the coded language of Brussels than his political representative. In other words, it needs to be a flagrant breach of national jurisdiction before anyone in the Member State begins to get worried. And even if this is the case, Brussels is capable of redrafting the same proposal in such a way that even professors in European law would have trouble deciphering its true meaning. It is doubtful whether the alarm bell procedure of the Treaty of Lisbon could ever be made to work properly.

European parliamentarians are not really keen on the subsidiarity test. They dislike the idea that national MPs, if they are well briefed and react quickly, can torpedo Commission proposals. The MEPs see this as their task, once the proposal has reached the hemicycle in Strasbourg. Although it might be more accurate to say that they prefer to amend the proposal beyond recognition, rather than simply allow national MPs to blow it out of the water. In this sense, MEPs and national MPs are often rivals, especially if it is a matter of media attention.

Thus, there is little the European citizen can do about the scale of Brussels bureaucracy and the scope of its legislative activity. The Treaty of Lisbon will probably be the last treaty of its kind for a number of years. Its realisation – following the failure of the European Constitution and the 'no' vote in the Irish referendum – was so difficult, that it has temporarily dampened the enthusiasm for further change of this kind.

This means that the European Commission will keep its top-heavy framework of 27 Commissioners and 35 Directorates-General. The Court of Justice and the European Court of Auditors have undergone similar expansion, as have the Committee of the Regions and the Economic and Social Committee. The latter two organs offer little added value these days, but they are maintained, simply on the basis of the bureaucratic principle that an institution, once founded, should never be decommissioned.

The European Parliament now contains a massive 751 members. To keep them occupied, there are 22 parliamentary committees and numerous work groups, sub groups, intergroups and groups of an indeterminate nature. Put simply, there is an imbalance throughout the Union's structural organisation.

The citizen can in theory influence the working of this mastodon by casting his (or her) vote once very five years, but in reality this vote counts for very little. Thanks to the block voting of political groupings, there can be large majorities in the Parliament which actually represent a minority of the votes cast by the electorate.

On 25 February 2010, the Parliament voted to increase its own budget in order to recruit more personnel. 430 MEPs voted for the proposal, 117 were against and there were 58 abstentions. Europe is in the middle of the worst financial and economic crisis for a generation and every citizen from the Atlantic to the Baltic is being asked to make sacrifices and tighten their belts. And so what does the Parliament do to set a good example of fiscal responsibility? It increases its own budget – just like that! And for 2011? It hopes to receive a budget of 1.7 billion euros – an increase of 6.5%! One pet project of the European Parliament worth 2.5 million euros is the construction of the 'Museum of European History', in a park next to its colossal edifices. The project is chaired by Hans-Gert Pöttering, the last survivor of the first directly-elected parliament in 1979. Why does a parliament which has reached the age of 30 want to build a museum for the purposes of self-glorification and aggrandisement? Instead of creating its own museum, the European Parliament should direct its energies towards preventing the EU from being turned into a museum in ten years' time. Before we know it, Europe will be history!

And what on earth are the citizens of Europe supposed to think about this type of cavalier, self-congratulatory behaviour? It is tantamount to saying: 'The rules apply to everybody – except us'. Little wonder that the European electorate has lost all faith in its 'representative' body.

The only way to stop this bureaucratic growth and to force the EU to concentrate on its core tasks is to get the budget back under tight control. The national budgets of the Member States are under severe pressure, even in the 'wealthy' net payer lands such as Germany, the Netherlands, Sweden, Great Britain, Austria and, since recently, Belgium (or Flanders, to be more precise).

Even so, it is certain that in the near future the Union will seek to boost its own resources by suggesting the introduction of new indirect taxation at a Europe-wide level – a measure that will hit every European in his wallet or her purse. If they are allowed to get away with this, then it is difficult to see where things are ever likely to stop.

A European tax will be the green flag for unlimited European centrism, leading to an economically ineffective Europe, which will slowly be crushed to death beneath the weight of its own legislative provisions. It will signify the end of the old Europe of nation states and the beginning of a new Europe of micro-management and social engineering. Worst of all, the European tax will feed a system which already carries the seed of its own destruction within itself. The European Union and the Soviet Union are not the same. But if the European Union continues to be nothing more than a bureaucratised ideal, it will certainly suffer the same fate as the Soviet Union. Europe needs focus – and quickly.

The Treaty of Lisbon offers a possible avenue for direct democratic action, although this is probably not what the architects of the treaty had in mind. It is called the European Citizens' Initiative (ECI). A minimum of one million citizens from nine member states can request the Commission to formulate a proposal on a matter which, in the opinion of the citizens, still needs to be addressed. Prior to the ECI, the initiators have to demonstrate that there is sufficient support within Europe: the Commission proposal requires the supporting signatures of 300,000 citizens from at least three EU Member States.

In theory, it is possible to suggest within this framework that a proposal be made to limit European bureaucracy, with its associated micro-management and spending mechanisms, so that the EU can once again focus on its core tasks in a manner that is less financially oppressive for the Member States and their citizens. If not, an unwieldy European Union will collapse under its own weight, turning the European continent into a provincial museum. What is the tool to sharpen focus? As always, it is money: the fuel of all bureaucracies.

A European Citizens' Initiative might recommend that the budget for the 2013-2020 period continues to be based on a maximum level of 1% of European GDP, with no increase of own resources.

The European project has resulted in the 'Europeanisation' of many sectors of activity, but so far this has not been the case with the taxpayers in Europe. They still have a national frame of reference. In view of the EU's plans to tax them directly in the near future, this could be to their disadvantage. Once tax-payers in Europe have understood the wicked fiscal schemes of Brussels, it will be too late. In the EU there are 16 national or regional associations of taxpayers. With the prospect of a budget debate about Europe-wide taxation, it is advisable that these associations should also organise themselves more vigorously on a Europe-wide basis – perhaps through an effective lobby of taxpayers' interests. After all, it is the taxpayers who fund the European budget, via their national contributions and the VAT levy. And if they want to address the EU's political bureaucratic machinery, they will also have to 'think European'.

I myself founded a taxpayers association in Belgium and the Netherlands (VlaNeTax) to put these issues on the political agenda, in cooperation with the think tank Libera! (www.vlanetax.eu)

I intend VlaNeTax to be the initial launching pad for a citizen's initiative to collect firstly 300,000 supporting signatures to demonstrate EU-wide endorsement and subsequently, in the framework of the official European Citizens' Initiative, at least the one million signatures necessary to appeal to the Commission not to introduce new EU taxes or to increase existing ones. As suggested above, the major objective of the tax-payers lobby could be to ensure the restriction of the budget for the 2013-2020 period to a maximum of 1% of European GDP. Over a seven year period, this still amounts to nearly one trillion euros. That is more than enough.

The website www.noeutax.eu will be the rallying point for this European Citizens' Initiative, both by providing the public, the media and the politicians with information, and for collecting the signatures. If the EU expects the citizens of Europe to tighten their belts, then there is no reason why it cannot do the same itself.

A European lobby of taxpayers is urgently needed, for the simple reason that the debate about the budget for 2013-2020 starts this year. In other words, the Commission will soon be making its first proposal. The sooner the taxpayers become active, the better – and happily the Treaty of Lisbon has shown the way. The longer they wait, the more likely that they will be faced with a European tax as a *fait accompli*. The taxpayers cannot rely on the European Parliament to secure their best interests, and so they must do it themselves.

In fact, the Parliament sees the European citizen as little more than a source of further income. On 10 March 2010, the MEPs voted on a proposal to assess the introduction of a tax on financial transactions. More than one group in the parliament feels that the banks and the public should pay a contribution on each financial transaction they make, such as loans, mortgages, transfers, or even possibly smaller cash withdrawals. The money – and believe me, it could amount to a very substantial sum – would be used for development aid and climate policy. The fact that development aid seldom helps and that climate policy is based on incorrect information seems not to be a relevant consideration.

The proposal approving research upon the new tax was passed with 561 votes for, 80 votes against and 17 abstentions. It looks as if the taxpayers of Europe need to get a move on – otherwise they will miss the boat.

The European Commission and the European Parliament are locked into the logic of 'more and more'. The Treaty of Lisbon proudly proclaimed: 'Citizens are represented at the Union level by the European Parliament.' But how and, if so, to what extent? The European Parliament wants ever higher expenditure and the Treaty of Lisbon invested them with the powers which can make this possible. The majority of the MEPs are firmly convinced that a European tax is a perfect way to bring the citizens closer to Europe. But it is very doubtful whether the citizens themselves see it that way! This is why an initiative launched by European citizens against a European tax would be of great symbolic and political importance. It is time for the people to speak. Taxpayers of Europe unite!

Of course, the system already has arguments prepared to counter this eventuality. Such as: 'Europe needs more money if it wants to remain a global player on the world stage.' A citizens' initiative on this particular matter would also be labelled as 'anti-European' (an old favourite reproach), not to mention 'egotistical' and 'nationalistic'.

But these arguments are easy to rebuff. The European Union is not even capable of managing its existing budget, let alone a much bigger one. It fails to use all of the funding allocated to it, and lives – in contrast to its member states – in a permanent state of budgetary underspending. To put it bluntly, the EU is not able to spend the money available and still it wants more!

Consider the report of the Commission with regard to financial and budgetary management for the year 2008. The approved budget for numerous lines of expenditure was not fully spent. The report pretends, for example, that the European Social Fund (ESF) used 97% of its allocated funding – but this is just a book-keeping trick. Within its budget containing a payment appropriation of 10.8 billion, the ESF transfers the sum of 1.615 billion out of the budget line through an annual 'budgetary amendment'. If we include the effect of other similar budgetary amendments, we arrive at an actual expenditure figure of just 8.8 billion euros. In other words, the real implementation rate of the ESF budget was close to 80%, and not 97%, as the report would have us believe. The fund was therefore unable to find a useful purpose for a fifth of the funding allocated to it.

And the picture is much the same for the European Fund for Regional Development (EFRD). In 2008, the original figure for the fund's committed credits – the amounts appropriated for projects – stood at 27.5 billion euros. The EFRD could not spend all that money. Finally, an amount of 22.9 billion euros remained as payment appropriations, of which subsequently 1.485 billion euros was transferred out of the budget line through a budgetary amendment. So, the spent amount was 21.4 billion euros. But the report – once again following 'amendments' – states that the implementation rate was 100%, when in reality it was much lower.

During the past decade, both these funds – the ESF and the EFRD – have had problems in using the funding allocated to them on an annual basis, whereas their annual budget continued to rise each year. In 2000, just 78% of the committed amount was spent. In 2001, this figure dropped to just 68%, before recovering back to 74% in 2002. But even then, this is just three-quarters of the anticipated amount.

There are various reasons for the shortfalls, the most important of which are: the unpredictable number of projects; the difficulty of matching projects to the increasingly complex economic-political criteria; co-funding from the Member States; and regular bureaucratic inertia. Whatever the excuse, the figures for recent years confirm that there is a 'structural underspending problem' in several key areas of European budgetary policy.

Believe it or not, but some funds are in an even worse position. In 2008, the Cohesion Fund had payment appropriations amounting to 6.7 billion euros, but in the course of the year some 1.435 billion euros were transferred out of the budget line. Consequently, the fund only managed to use 5.2 billion euros of its allocated funding, whereas the EU once again has attempted to claim that the implementation rate was 100%. The European Globalisation Fund carried over a reserve of 451 million euros at the end of 2008, while the Seventh Framework Programme for Research and Development only managed to implement 84% of its funding. The External Action budget line achieved a 90% average implementation rate during the period

2000-2006, with the Common Agricultural Fund scoring best of all at about 92%.

The European Commission's report on budgetary financial management 2009 reflects the newly introduced budget architecture (very clever accounting techniques indeed!) but the general picture remains the same: the EU still cannot spend all the money it has, while claiming close to 100 percent implementation rates nevertheless. Especially in the big European funds, the difference between commitment and payment appropriations is even more striking.

During the negotiations for the 2007-2013 budgetary period, both the European Commission and the European Parliament argued that an annual EU budget of 1% of EU-GDP was 'wholly inadequate' for the implementation of a credible policy programme. But in reality, the EU has shown itself to be consistently unable to spend even this amount. In the major European funds, average budget implementation hovers somewhere between 80% and 90%.

This is the clearest possible proof – the 'smoking gun' – that Brussels does not need more money, unless they are planning to throw sacks of the stuff through the windows of the ivory towers. There is no justification whatsoever for a new indirect EU tax. On the contrary, there is every reason to restrict the EU budget, in order to force the Union to refocus on its core tasks and display self-restraint in budgetary matters, as the average taxpayer is supposed to do. In its reply to my written question (2560/10) the Commission admits that in 2008 'payments turned out to be much below the budget' and the unspent sum of 4,5 billion euro was subsequently returned to the member states.

This is therefore not an anti-European message, but rather a pro-European appeal to the taxpayers of the continent, who have the power to bring about this change – refocus the European integration process – through the mechanisms foreseen in the Treaty of Lisbon. But they need to act today – tomorrow will be too late.

7

THE EVER DEADLIER SINS

The Brussels Tower of Babel is governed by seven illusions, which continue to create an ever-widening gap between the rhetoric of the European Union and the unpalatable truth. The extent of this gulf is concealed by the use of semantic language, long declarations and high-flown idealism. How do they see themselves? The European institutional elite is the vanguard of European integration. They show the way, and the people must follow. Europe is a source of 'great good' and the 'more Europe' they can create, the happier the people will be. Europe also plays a crucial role in the world, where it once again marches in the vanguard. The European method works, both within the EU and beyond.

This is the self-image. But in reality the European elite are deluded. Their vision is blurred by seven intellectual misconceptions – seven deadly sins, if you like – which lead to repeated disappointment, a need for constant recalibration, the search for 'anti-European' scapegoats, the creation of new symbols and the development of new institutions, which cost ever increasing sums of money. In this manner, the European Union has become trapped in its own rhetoric – a rhetoric that the people now no longer believe. The legitimacy of the European project is being increasingly undermined.

What are these seven deadly sins?

1. The nation state is finished.
The bureaucrats of the European Union, particularly those in the European Commission and the European Parliament, see the European Member States, in particular nation states, as en-

tities that will gradually diminish in importance. They are the exponents of harmful nationalist ideas and dangerous self-interest, and they must be tamed by the European elite. Viewed from the European perspective, the nation state is 'provincial' and 'narcissistic'. They need to be absorbed as quickly as possible into a wider European entity, which has the interests of all the continent's peoples at heart. To ease the transition, people can retain some of the symbols of the 'old ways' – German *Lederhosen*, Finnish folk dances, Dutch clogs, Italian operas and Spanish bullfights – although this last one may be in doubt, given the Union's commitment to animal welfare. In moral, political and intellectual terms, the European Union is far superior to the nation states, and the European elite is the guardian of European values and ambition.

The reality is very different. People's need for a national identity is greater than ever, and it is a subject of active discussion in many of the EU's member states. All over the continent, European citizens are asking themselves who they really are and what values their societies represent. Faced with the effects of continuing globalisation, there is a growing need to focus on our own individual identities more sharply. This is certainly true in secularised Western Europe, where religion no longer offers the supposed certainties of life. This need for a sharper focus has been heightened by the mass immigration of people from different political, cultural and religious backgrounds. In Western Europe this had already led to a clash of ideologies. Constitutional rights, such as freedom of expression, religious tolerance and sexual equality, have now been shown to have only a so-called relative value, since many of the newcomers give different interpretations to these key aspects of society. Whole districts in European cities have changed in both mood and appearance, so that many European citizens are now afflicted by a sense of inner alienation, a kind of *Überfremdung*. This raises many questions, but the European elite can offer no answers – and no real alternatives but to preach the gospel of the multicultural society.

The concept of a 'European identity' cannot serve as a substitute, because no such identity exists. There is no 'European people', with a common language and a common public opinion. True, we do share a common cultural heritage based on the Judaic-Christian tradition. This European culture has resulted in the primacy of values such as civil freedoms, the separation of church and state, democratic and constitutional rights, and equality between men and women. Centuries of history, the struggles for social and religious freedoms, and the hard experience of (world) wars has provided every part of the continent with cultural building blocks, which we now find reflected in our social and economic systems at national level, and of which the democratic and constitutional state is the political expression.

But a common European culture is not the same as a common European identity. Instead, the Europeans have built a series of national identities based on their common cultural heritage. These national identities are constructed around a community with a common language, common historical experiences, common cultural perceptions, a common public opinion and common customs and traditions. The Finns and the Greeks are both Europeans, but they are as different as chalk and cheese. They both have different political-cultural software. The same is true for the Danish and the Spanish, the Irish and the Latvians, the Portuguese and the Austrians, etc. Europe is a finely-meshed net of sensitivities, and you don't need to travel very far anywhere in the continent before you are confronted by this fact.

For example, the Dutch have more in common with the Germans than they would like to admit. And they have less in common with the Dutch-speaking Flemings than most of them believe. As a 'cross-border' member of the European Parliament, I know what I am talking about. Believe me, national identities are very different. As a result, the political framework of Europe is still based on the nation states that reflect these national identities. States with no real feeling of nationality – such as Belgium – are the exception rather than the rule. But one thing is certain: there is no European identity, and so we must be careful not to force people to accept the development of a European political entity which has no common foundations on which its structure can be built. However, the European elite misguidedly believes that a European identity can be created, but this would be as superficial, if not artificial, as the old Soviet identity, and would encourage a similar mentality. Political structures built on wishful thing are like the biblical houses built on sand: they inevitably collapse.

Moreover, it is no longer possible for the European Union to strive for an extended federal structure, since the Treaty of Lisbon effectively concentrated power in the hands of the European Council, which comprises the various government leaders of the member countries. Henceforth, the European Council will set the guidelines and there is now a President of Europe to ensure that the Council's instructions – in particular, the instructions of the larger and more powerful member states – are followed.

The political balance of power has shifted from the Commission to the Council, so that the former is now more involved with the implementation of policy, rather than solely determining its initiation. The Treaty of Lisbon also gave more power to the European Parliament, and the Parliament – notwithstanding the strengthened position of the Council – still sees itself as the guardian of the federal ideal. Together with the Commission, it is an ardent believer in the existence of the European identity, which it seeks to facilitate through the creation of supranational institutions invested with supranational competences. As such, they perpetuate the illusion of the first deadly sin.

The European Union can only obtain legitimacy from the peoples of Europe if it profiles itself as an organisation where nation states pool parts of their national sovereignty in clearly-defined fields of policy in order to create an added value that works to the benefit of all the Member States. The nation state must continue to provide the overall frame of reference, because this is the frame of reference within which the citizens of Europe think.

The Member States must therefore determine the policy domains where this pooling can be most effective, rather than accepting the top-down imposition of policy by the European elite in Brussels, who believe that they – and they alone – know what is best for the people. However, the people identify with their own nation states, not with the European elite. This means that the states must form the basis for the EU, and not the political-bureaucratic elite. The EU can only succeed if it becomes a United Europe of States and not a United States of Europe. Wrong analysis leads to wrong results – which in politics inevitably lead to disaster.

2. 'More Europe' is the magical solution for all problems.
Every problem in the European Union is labelled as a 'European' problem. To solve these problems, the European elite devise 'European' solutions that always result in more bureaucratic power, more legislation and more institutions.

The concept of subsidiarity is a carrot dangled in front of critics, to distract their attention and to keep them happy. The unavoidable consequence of 'more Europe' is a larger and stronger bureaucracy: it has the same effect as the use of steroids in the world of sport. 'More Europe' is a concept that works horizontally, so that its field of application is constantly being extended. A single incident or problem can be used to claim an entire field of policy as a 'European domain'. The European Parliament demands new initiatives and the Commission produces them with conveyor-belt efficiency. The train is set in motion and soon develops a momentum that is impossible to stop.

As a result, Europe is now doing so much in so many different areas that there are very few people who know where its powers begin or (more importantly) where they end. The European Parliament determines the length of maternity leave throughout Europe and then, once it has got its finger in the social policy pie, insists that other European social initiatives must follow. The same phenomenon also occurs in culture and education. Even policy domains which are largely the province of the national governments are coming increasingly under the influence of the European decision-making process. How should sex education be taught in Lithuania? The European anti-discrimination directives will show them the way!

There is a permanent proliferation of 'more Europe'. The EU attempts to concentrate on so many side issues that it has lost sight of its core tasks, where more integration is needed.

The Internal Market has still not been fully implemented and the Commission is too scared to haul Member States before the Court of Justice to demand compliance with its own internal market legislation. The Commission prefers a 'mutual dialogue' with Member States, which gives them an easy way out of implementing agreed rules through endless procrastination. The Services Directive (about 70 percent of the EU economy consists somehow of services) has been emasculated by taking out the "country of origin" principle which is the guiding tenet in internal market legislation: a service allowed in one Member State should be allowed in all Member States. Now, it is harder for service providers to launch cross-border activities. They may be required to obtain licences from national bureaucracies, which creates too many costs for SME's. Who took the "country of origin" principle out? The European Parliament! It turned the service directive into a car without an engine, harming the economic growth the European economy so desperately needs. In this way, the European Parliament even impoverishes Europeans.

At the same time, the people watch helplessly as the euro comes under increasing pressure, because the provisions of the Union's own Stability and Growth Pact are flouted with impunity. The Commission knew months, if not years, ago that the crisis in Greece would eventually explode, but it lacked the courage to intervene. It did nothing, for fear of offending the Greeks. In other words, 'more Europe' has gradually become an excuse for failing to enforce the political discipline necessary for the good administration of Europe. The European elite must learn – and learn quickly – that if they fail to implement their core tasks successfully, all their other efforts will be of marginal value. The citizens of Europe will not be overly concerned about the problems of sex education in Lithuania if the euro is collapsing in value around their ears, ruining tens of thousands of investors, savers and pensioners in the process. A reform of the Stability and Growth Pact must contain an exit procedure; if not, one country can contaminate the entire euro-zone which will break up as a result.

3. Micro-management is necessary.
Now that the European Union has managed to take over most fields of policy responsibility – and is therefore in a position to

make 'European policy' – the legislative process is deepened via micro-management. The result is a series of major legislative initiatives on a Europe-wide scale, which define in detail how everything must be done, and by whom. The Habitat Directive is a good example of this tactic in practice, since it works in both breadth and depth. As a consequence of the directive, Brussels has got its claws into habitat zones in all the member states and there is no way that the states can force the bureaucrats to release their grip. Much the same is true in the chemical industry as a result of the REACH directive, even though the directive is so complex that it is no longer workable. The story seems likely to be repeated in the financial sector, where the new structure of supervision attempts to go so far in terms of depth that the cumulative effect is one of overregulation, which will cause investors and entrepreneurs to look elsewhere. If it is disconnected from global financial markets, the EU will turn the European capital market into a self-inflicted Sahara; and all because the rules are sacred, no matter what their consequences.

In the previous century, the Soviet Planning Bureau used to set a staggering 20 million prices each year – or at least attempted to. The result of this near impossible situation was empty shelves, no choice for the consumers (on the rare occasions that there were products to buy) and a production process that owed more to the Middle Ages than to the 20th century.

With its own version of micro-management, the European Union must be very careful that it does not create a similar effect. The problem, however, is that the European elite is simply fond of micro-management, because it is the very essence of bureaucracy. This is another area where the Commission has already gone too far, but the Parliament wants to go even further. The Parliament should act as a brake on micro-management, but actually serves to encourage it. In fact, the Parliament is no longer satisfied with its role as a legislator of policy; it wants to become a co-initiator of policy as well!

Since a lot of micro-management currently stems from the environmental sector, the Green lobby – in particular its wide network of EU-sponsored NGOs – requires closer inspection. The Green lobby is more powerful than the agricultural lobby ever was. The latter was deeply embedded in ruling Christian Democratic parties, along with its corporatist structure of professional organisations. As a result, the agricultural lobby was politically untouchable for years, even when technology turned agriculture into agro-industry. The sector produced enormous surpluses and it took decades to rein in the wrong-headed policies that generated them. The EU not only produced food, it also destroyed it voluntarily.

Nowadays, the Green lobby creates similar effects: micro-management and social engineering. It is politically well embedded, not only in Green parties but in most ruling parties. Green is good! But the Greens are not always right. The Green lobby needs to be reined in by a countervailing power of critics both in politics and media. Green NGOs should receive less EU subsidies (taxpayers' money, after all) and rely to a much larger extent on individual contributions from citizens. If checked, the Green lobby will create the same sort of disastrous policy effects as the agricultural lobby did in the 1970s and 1980s. Whether the Greens like it or not, Europe needs a competitive industrial basis to provide work and income for people.

4. The European Parliament represents the citizens.

This is highly questionable, for the simple reason that the concept of a 'Europe of citizens' does not exist. It presupposes that the citizen has something to say and the right to say it, but this is not the case. Even if the citizens attempt to voice their discontent by not voting in European elections, Brussels concludes that this is an expression of silent consent for their policies.

In a Europe with more than 500 million citizens, there is inevitably a wide range of opinions, but you will not find this reflected in the European Parliament, where there is only one opinion: 'more Europe, and more money for more Europe!' There is no opposition to create a sense of balance, and those who question the wisdom of the prevailing policy are instantly labelled as 'anti-European'.

The European Parliament should be the institution that protects Europe's citizens against excessive taxation and excessive overregulation, which work to the detriment of both individuals and companies. But it does precisely the opposite: it encourages both these processes and even intensifies them. The European Parliament will only become a true (i.e. representative) parliament if it recognises the right of opposition and allows debate to flow from the different opinions which abound in Europe. As the German Constitutional Court rightly pointed out, the current European Parliament is a parliament in Europe, rather than the Parliament of Europe.

5. A European tax.

In the philosophy of the European elite, 'more money for Europe' is a matter of simple logic. The European Union does more and more for its peoples, and therefore needs more money to make this possible. 'Doing good' is an expensive business. For this reason, the current EU budget of 141 billion euros is seen as inadequate for all the 'ambitious' plans which the Union wishes to implement. Unfortunately, the Member States are finding it harder and harder to pay their contributions in full. National budgets no longer balance and national debt levels are increasing rapidly.

Therefore, the EU now thinks that it would be better to have a new level of indirect taxation paid directly to Brussels, so that the taxpayers can get 'real' value for their money. This, so the argument goes, will also help to make them feel more attached to the European ideal.

This is the most dangerous of the seven deadly sins of the European elite. To begin with, the rate of the new European tax (or charge, or levy, or whatever you want to call it) will rise very quickly – and the citizens of Europe will have no effective means to resist. They will simply have to pay up and shut up. The European politicians will claim that this new tax replaces equivalent taxes at national level, which will be abolished. But who are they trying to kid?

In the current economic and financial situation, national ministers of finance need every eurocent they can raise. They are in no position to scrap lucrative sources of revenue – even if they wanted to. Besides, the European Union doesn't really need a European tax, since it has problems spending all the money which it is already allocated. Most of the major European institutions and funds report annual underspends. So where is the need for a European tax?

In fact, a European tax may even spell the end of Europe. It would allow the bureaucracy to grow still further and would result in a massive increase in legislation, to such an extent that the peoples of Europe would probably pull the plug on the European project. In this sense, the fight against the European tax is also a fight for the future of Europe – but a Europe that refocuses on its core tasks. The taxpayers of Europe must be prepared to defend themselves. The launching of a citizens' initiative could be the first step towards correcting the distorted growth of the Union. But in this respect, the citizens are on their own: they can expect no support from the European Parliament.

6.   Europe is a global player.
This deadly sin is more understandable, but is nevertheless based on wishful thinking. Europe has the potential to be a global player, but only on the basis of a strongly developed internal market, a credible euro and a dynamic economy, with innovative production, a well-motivated workforce, cultural opti-

mism and leaders with vision. Sadly, none of these conditions currently exists.

The internal market is still not strong enough, while the euro is presently rocking on its foundations, thanks to the irresponsible financial behaviour of Greece. Innovation is still more an American characteristic than a European one, and many companies have switched their operations to the other side of the Atlantic. For example, Europe's pharmaceutical R&D sector has moved *en masse* to the US, because of the difficulty of securing international property rights in Europe. In similar vein, Europe's chemical industry is coming under increasing pressure because of the EU's unrealistic climate policy.

Jobs in all sectors are being lost at an alarming rate, and for most people the European dream has been reduced to early retirement in Spain or the South of France, hopefully before the pension fund runs out. The welfare state mentality is undermining Europe's entrepreneurial spirit and is reducing the old continent to the status of a regional player (at best). A global player needs to do more than give money to the ruling elites of developing countries or to act as a shining (but wholly unrealistic) moral example in the field of climate policy. The EU likes to talk of a European defence policy, but how many divisions does it have ready to take the field? Europe is a paper tiger and is only capable of fulfilling a symbolic role. Perhaps this is just as well, since the present generation of European citizens is no longer prepared to sanction anything. The people are pacifistic and prefer appeasement to the defence of legitimate rights.

Afghanistan – a war sanctioned by resolutions of the UN Security Council and NATO – is a bridge too far for most Europeans. They want to bring their troops home, and are prepared to leave it to the Americans to struggle on alone. Worse still, they will then quite happily accuse the Americans of aggression and arrogant behaviour. The Europeans are too impassive, if not downright lazy, to turn Europe into a global power, and public opinion is too indifferent to care.

European leaders make fine speeches and noble gestures, but these are just a means to hide the real weakness of their position. Europe wants to be 'a force for good' in the world. In contrast, China wants to conquer as many markets as possible, and is prepared to be as hard as it takes to achieve this goal. The Americans, the Russians and the Indians are no different. Europe may preach 'kindness' and 'goodness', but would be unwise to expect others to do likewise.

7. It's always somebody else's fault!

If something goes wrong in Europe, for whatever reason, the Europeans are always ready to pass the blame on to someone else. This is easy to understand in psychological terms, since they have been blaming each other as nation states for centuries. The French blamed the Germans (and vice versa), the Poles blamed the Russians, and the British blamed the whole continent! This mechanism still exists: it is just that the names of the guilty parties have been changed. Consider the recent crisis in Greece. In essence, the Greeks drew up a series of fraudulent budgets, which resulted in a huge national debt, the repayments for which they were unable to make. The country was plunged into financial crisis (where it still remains), but who gets the blame?

The 'speculators' of Goldman Sachs, who helped the Greeks with credit default swaps, which artificially reduced the overall level of their debts. Or blame is allocated to the (American) credit rating agencies after downgrading the ratings of Portuguese and Spanish debt obligations. However, it is not the market spreading monetary contagion but the EU's impotence to police the Eurozone vigorously and to act decisively in case the rules are infringed upon. The European method of indefinite talking and poor enforcement undermines confidence in the common currency. And most amazingly, some countries pursuing lax monetary policies over the past decade blame Germany for their current plight, whereas the federal republic is the irreplaceable anchor of the euro altogether.

The EU now plans to take action against credit default swaps in its battle against 'irresponsible speculation', which has suddenly become a source of great public evil. But who built up the massive Greek debts? The Greeks! Not Goldman-Sachs. Did Goldman-Sachs force the Greeks to accept credit default swaps? No, they asked for them voluntarily. The Greek political class is behaving like an alcoholic who blames his addiction on the barkeeper who keeps serving him.

When the wider financial crisis broke at the end of 2008, the blame was placed on hedge funds, which had been used without comment for more than a decade, but were now all of a sudden an evil manifestation of locust capitalism. Under pressure from Germany, France and the European Parliament, the European Commission produced a draft directive against all forms of venture capital, including the fairly safe private equity. But hedge funds had not caused the crisis. Overnight they were turned into villains.

Europeans share one characteristic: whenever things go pear-shaped, their first instinct is to look around for a convenient scapegoat. But what they really need to do is to accept the facts for what they are, communicate them clearly – and then take a long, hard look at themselves in the mirror. The weaknesses which are currently making things so difficult for Europe were also created by Europe – and by nobody else. Who is actively threatening Europe? The Americans? The Chinese? The Russians? The Arabs? None of them, of course. The biggest threat to the future of Europe is a European system estranged from reality.

The coming ten years will be of crucial importance for Europe. As Americans say: 'If you're not at the table, you're on the menu.' Will Europe be 'subject' or 'object' in the new world order? A Europe which does nothing more than talk about the accumulation of rights and social protection is following the path to destruction, which will result in the bankruptcy of its political, economic and cultural systems. This will already be evident in ten years time. The economic basis of Europe is already being eroded, so that the situation may worsen to a level only known to the older pre-war generation: being old means being poor. Europe's social fabric is also under pressure, with millions of immigrants living in ghetto districts in most of Europe's major cities.

These are not situations that can be solved with 'more rights'. There need to be corresponding obligations. Europe must urgently find a tenable economic basis for its social structures. The European dream of 'early retirement' is a Europe without a future.

Europe needs to work – not to stop working. Education should be used to teach, and not simply to moralise. Space must be created for more entrepreneurship, with lower tax rates for business – even if this also means fewer 'rights' for the workforce. Perseverance and performance, independence and innovation: these are the qualities which are needed to save Europe, but they have almost become terms of abuse anno 2010. The Europeans have a culture of envy, which is little more than the quickest route to equality in poverty. Performance is not rewarded, but is resented: 'If I can't have it, then no one else is going to have it either!" Perhaps Europeans can learn a thing or two from the American dream, with its focus on optimism and self-realisation.

During the coming ten years, Europe will need to innovate in order to survive. It will not be easy, and the mentality of the welfare state will be of no use in this difficult struggle. 'More Europe' and a European tax are not the solutions. They are placebos, which will only serve to hide the real symptoms of our disease. Europe must encourage its creative spirits. Such spirits do exist, but they must be sought out, cherished and supported.

Have you ever heard a European government leader say any of this to the electorate? There is no point in the President of the Commission saying it, since he is not subject to the democratic process. The same is true of the President of the Council. The members of the European Parliament would never be able to get the words across their lips, and besides, the voters stopped listening to them a long time ago.

No, the government leaders in the Member States are the only people who can say it, and say it with effect. Will they dare to tell the hard and uncompromising truth? Are they scared that they might not be re-elected? Perhaps they are – just look at the approval ratings of the reform-minded French President Sarkozy. But there is more at stake than a handful of political careers. Europe faces a crisis far greater than the people actually realise. If we're not at the table in 2020, we will indeed be on the menu. And if the leaders of Europe fail to tell this message – and tell it now – then the continent of Europe will miss the train of history.